ISTANBUL
Gate to the Orient

by Turhan Can

Translated by Gaye Tınaztepe

Founder of modern Turkey

Mustafa Kemal Atatürk
1881-1938

TABLE of CONTENTS

GEOGRAPHICAL POSITION

Istanbul, the most heavily populated city in Turkey, has after the last census 10 million inhabitants. Istanbul is located on the 41 st degree of the northern latitude, somewhat like Naples. However, the climate is cooler because of the north winds, and at summer time it is very enjoyable along the coast.

Istanbul is the only city in the world that stretches onto two continents. The main part of the city stands on the south-eastern tip of Europe, and is separated from its suburbs in Asia by the Bosphorus. The Golden Horn then divides the European section of the city into two parts: Ancient **Stambul** to the south, and **Galata** and **Beyoğlu** (the old Pera) to the north. Finally the old Skutari (now **Üsküdar**), is located on the Asian side of the Bosphorus.

This fascinating city stretching along the shores of the Marmara Sea, the Golden Horn and the Bosphorus, has been the seat of two empires and the centre of art and science for several hundred years.

HISTORY

The settlement of Semistra must have been established at the end of the Golden Horn in 1000 B.C. Later on, the residents must have esttled on the acropolis above Seraglio point where the settlement Lygos had already been inhabited since the 9th century B.C.

The legend calls Byzas from Megara, the founder of Byzantium, and gives the year 667 B.C. as when a colony on the acropolis was established.

From the beginning of its history Byzantium was an important centre of commerce. In the Persian war against the Skythes, the city placed its ships at the Persian king darius disposal for him to cross the Bosphorus. The city remained under Persian control until the battle of Plataea in 479 B.C. Then the Spartan general Pausanias, ruled the city as he wished. In 196 A.D. the Roman Emperor Septimius Severus conquered the city and destroyed it. It's believed that the emperor rebuilt the city at his son's request. In the process he enlarged it with a new surrounding wall and built the Hippodrome and palaces. In the year 324 A.D. Licinius, the rival of Emperor Constantine I, fled to Byzantium. Constantine followed him and defeated him in Chrysopolis (Üsküdar). The city excited Constantine so much, that he declared it the capital of the Roman Empire in the year 330 A.D.

Constantine named the city after himself and it became Constantinople. He decided to reconstruct it completely in order to create a New Rome. He enclosed the city with a larger wall complex and had palaces and churches built. His successor Theodosius I ordered the non-Christian temples to be torn down, and he divided the empire between his two sons. Honorius ruled the West and Arcadius the East. The western part of the empire was ended by the German general Odoakar, whereas the eastern part of existed till the conquest of Istanbul by the Turks in 1453. The fall of the western part in fact, marked the beginning of the East Roman Empire, i.e. the emperor in Istanbul was the only heir to the Roman Empire.

The Golden Age of Istanbul was that of Emperor Justinian's reign (527-565). At the time of his death the borders of Byzantium streched from the Euphrates to Gibralter. However, the Golden Age didn't last long. During the 7th and 8th centuries the city was assaulted by Avars, Persians and Arabs. The year 754 is important from the point of view that, these Moslems influenced iconoclasm, which forbade the worship of images. After the termination of iconoclasm the empire achieved its second Golden Age under the rule of Macedonian emperors (867-1057).

Later however, the defeat of the Byzantine army in the east (in Manzikert) in 1071, the existence of the Normans in the west, and the economical burden of the crusades weakened the empire considerably.

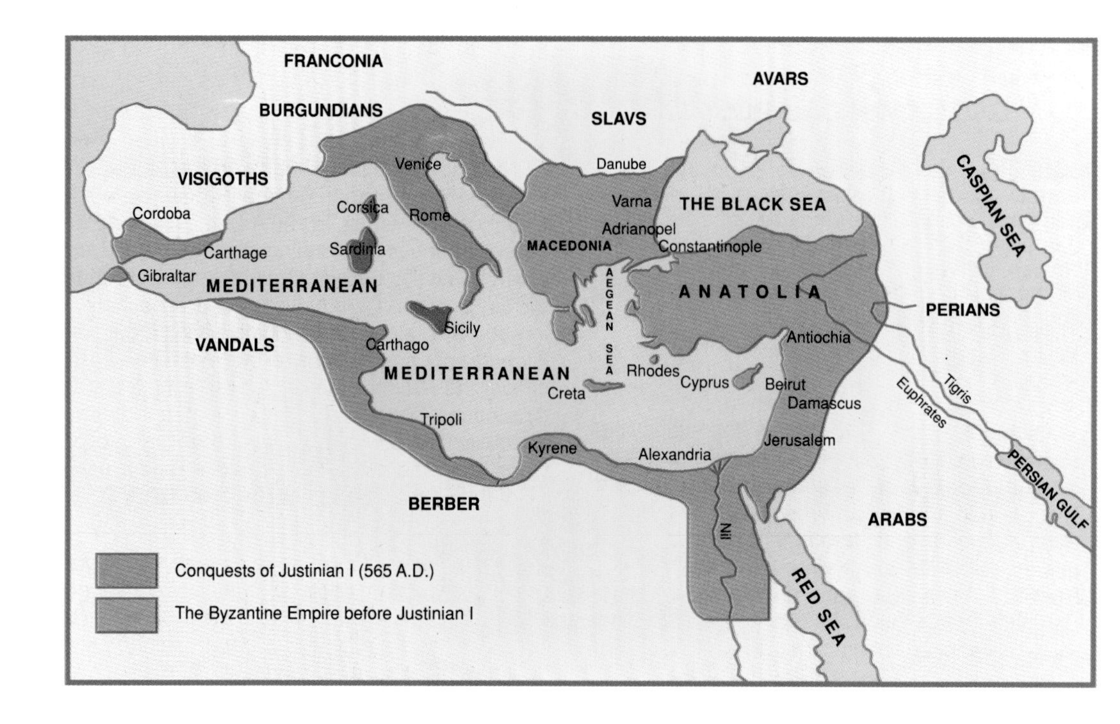

The objective of the Crusades changed after the Crusaders had seen the rich city of Constantinople. Instead of freeing the Holy Land from the Arabs, the Crusaders wanted to loot the rich city. In the year of 1204, the armies of the Fourth Crusade destroyed and sacked it, and a Latin Empire was founded in Istanbul (1204-1261). The Byzantine emperor fled to Nicaea (İznik), and established a semi-Byzantine empire, while a number of fugitives left for Trapezunt (Trabzon).

After the Latin Dynasty in Istanbul, the Palaelogus succeded to the Byzantine throne in 1261 and reigned until the city was conquered by the Turks in 1453. Following the conquest a new era began, and Istanbul became the capital of the Ottoman Empire remaining so for four hundred and seventy years (1453-1923).

After the conquest, the new capital was decorated with mosques, palaces, Turkish baths and fountains.During this age of expansion in the 16th century the empire reached a peak of power and of art. Its farthest borders were reached, the territory stretching from Persia in the east, to Vienna in the west, and from North Africa in the south to Russia in the north. The most powerful sultan of this era was Süleyman the Magnificent who stayed in power for forty six years (1520 - 1566). It was just pure coincidence and good fortune that Sinan, the most famous architect of the empire, who created over three hundred masterpieces, lived during Süleyman's rule. We are grateful to him for the most meaningful masterpieces of architecture in Istanbul.

Şüleyman's successor was Selim II whose mother, the second wife of Sultan Süleyman II, was called "Roxelane". Selim was lucky to inherit an extraordinarily well organized empire which made important progress in the fields of science and art. In the 17th and 18th centuries the sultans were influenced by their grand viziers and the janissaries, until the latter were crushed by Mahmut II in 1826,by executing thirty thousand of them in the Hippodrome.

In the 18th century, buildings were designed in baroque and rococo styles. The 19th century was full of disagreements with European countries. The Russians were a threat, nations in the Balkans wanted to declare their independence, and the Egyptians were advancing in Anatolia.

As a result of the Balkan War in 1911-1912 Greece and Bulgaria became independent. The

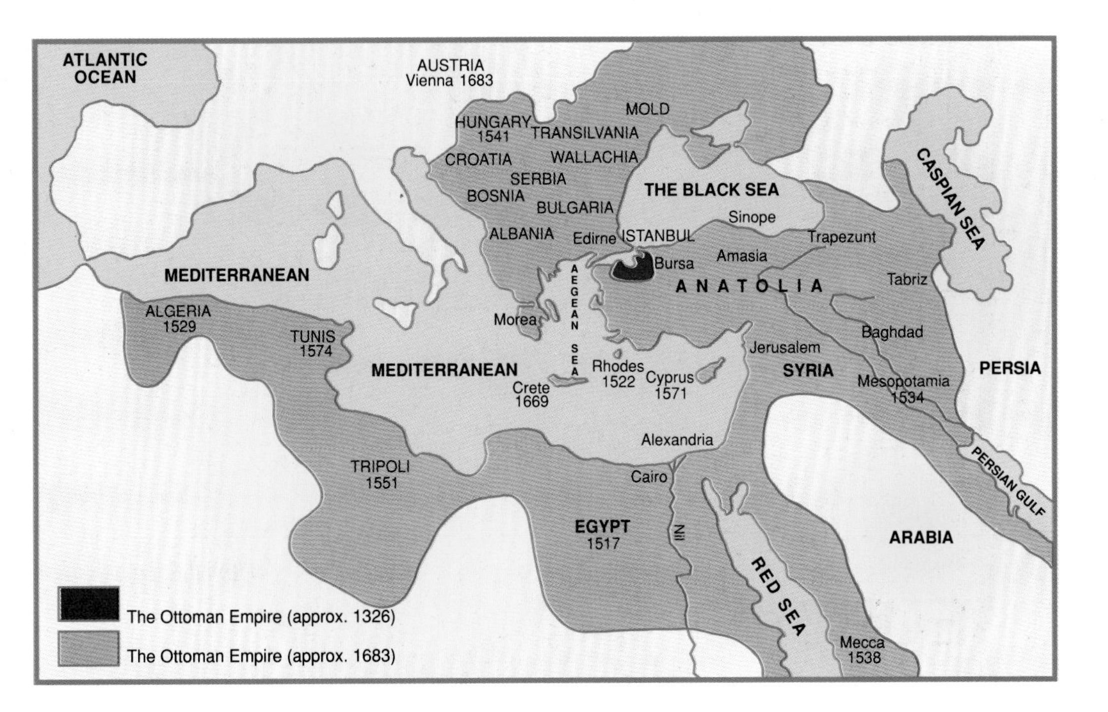

country found itself on the losing side in the First World War, after which the victorious Allies proceeded to divide up the remnants of the Ottoman Empire amongst themself. Alied troops occupied Istanbul and the Greeks landed in Smyrna (Izmir) with a plan to incorporate western Anatolia into Greater Greece. The French occupied southeastern Anatolia, and the Italians occupied the south. Turkey was saved by the efforts of its people who rebelled against this situation and started the War of Independence under the command of Mustafa Kemal Paşa (Atatürk). In 1922 the last of the invading Greeks were driven out of the country and the empire was dissolved. The last sultan, Mehmet VI was declared a rebel by Atatürk ant fled Turkey on an English war vessel. He died in San Remo in 1929. A nephew of the sultan was appointed caliph without any administrative power. On October 29th 1923 Atatürk laid the foundations of the Turkish Republic. He became the first president of the republic and took residence in Ankara. In 1924 the Caliphate was abolished; Caliph Abdülmecit left the country in the same year, and died in Nice in 1944.

In 1928 Atatürk started to introduce reforms to modernize Turkey (e.g. the Latin alphabet, the Gregorian calender, monogamy, the observance of sunday as a holiday, voting rights for women, the acquiring of surnames, and banning of the fez).

After Atatürk died 1938, Ismet Inönü was elected President. In the Second World War, Turkey stayed neutral until it declared war on Germany in 1945. In 1950 the Democrats won the election. Their leader "Celal Bayar" became the President, and "Adnan Menderes" the Prime Minister. In 1952 Turkey joined NATO. In 1960 the Menderes Administration was overthrown. The new president was General Gürsel, and the Prime Minister was Ismet Inönü. In 1965 the Justice Party came to power and Süleyman Demirel became Prime Minister. The military took-over again in 1971, then the leader the social democratic Republican People's Party, Ecevit, won the election in 1974. These two parties administered the country on and off during the following years until General Evren realized a military take-over on September 12th 1980. Until the elections on November 6th. 1983, the military stayed in power. After that the liberal Motherland Party has been governing the country. Since the elections on 20th. October 1991 the liberals and the social-democrats are administering the country.

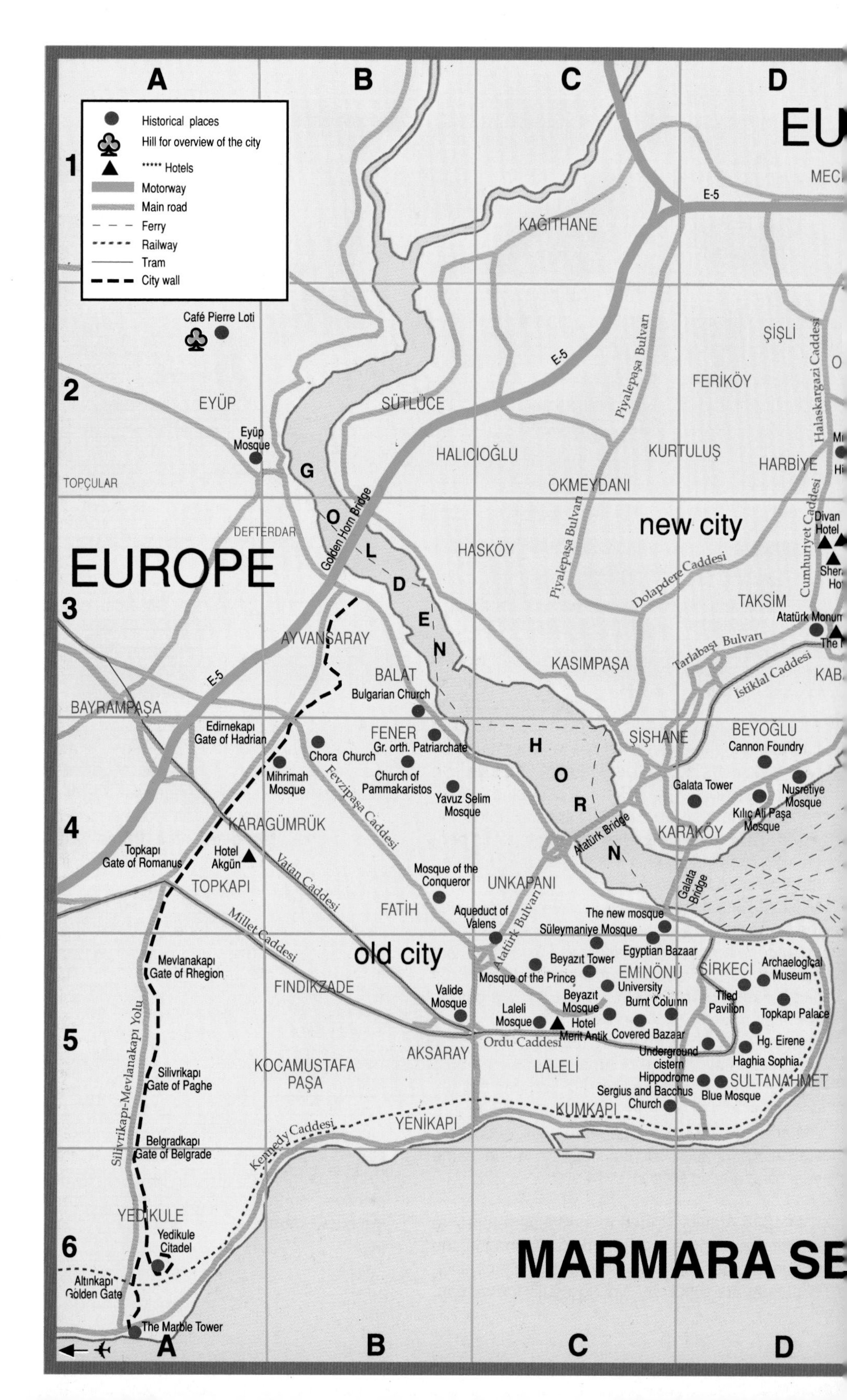

A
B
C
D
1
2
3
4
5
6
Historical places
Hill for overview of the city
***** Hotels
Motorway
Main road
Ferry
Railway
Tram
City wall
EUROPE
MARMARA SE
KAĞITHANE
E-5
ŞİŞLİ
FERİKÖY
KURTULUŞ
HARBİYE
OKMEYDANI
HALICIOĞLU
SÜTLÜCE
EYÜP
Eyüp Mosque
Café Pierre Loti
TOPÇULAR
DEFTERDAR
HASKÖY
new city
TAKSİM
Atatürk Monum
AYVANSARAY
BALAT
KASIMPAŞA
Bulgarian Church
BAYRAMPAŞA
Edirnekapı Gate of Hadrian
FENER
Gr. orth. Patriarchate
Chora Church
Mihrimah Mosque
Church of Pammakaristos
Yavuz Selim Mosque
ŞİŞHANE
BEYOĞLU
Cannon Foundry
Galata Tower
Nusretiye Mosque
Kılıç Ali Paşa Mosque
KARAKÖY
KARAGÜMRÜK
Topkapı Gate of Romanus
Hotel Akgün
TOPKAPI
Mosque of the Conqueror
UNKAPANI
FATİH
Aqueduct of Valens
Atatürk Bridge
Galata Bridge
Golden Horn Bridge
G O L D E N H O R N
The new mosque
Süleymaniye Mosque
Egyptian Bazaar
Beyazıt Tower
EMİNÖNÜ
SİRKECİ
Archaelogical Museum
old city
Mosque of the Prince
University
Beyazıt Mosque
Burnt Column
Tiled Pavilion
Topkapı Palace
Mevlanakapı Gate of Rhegion
FINDIKZADE
Valide Mosque
Laleli Mosque
Hotel Merit Antik
Covered Bazaar
Hg. Eirene
AKSARAY
Ordu Caddesi
Underground cistern
Haghia Sophia
Silivrikapı Gate of Paghe
KOCAMUSTAFA PAŞA
LALELİ
Hippodrome
SULTANAHMET
Sergius and Bacchus Church
Blue Mosque
KUMKAPI
YENİKAPI
Kennedy Caddesi
Belgradkapı Gate of Belgrade
Silivrikapı-Mevlanakapı Yolu
YEDİKULE
Yedikule Citadel
Altınkapı Golden Gate
The Marble Tower
Fevzipaşa Caddesi
Vatan Caddesi
Millet Caddesi
Atatürk Bulvarı
Piyalepaşa Bulvarı
Dolapdere Caddesi
Tarlabaşı Bulvarı
İstiklal Caddesi
Halaskargazi Caddesi
Cumhuriyet Caddesi
Divan Hotel
HARBİYE
KAB
MEC
EU

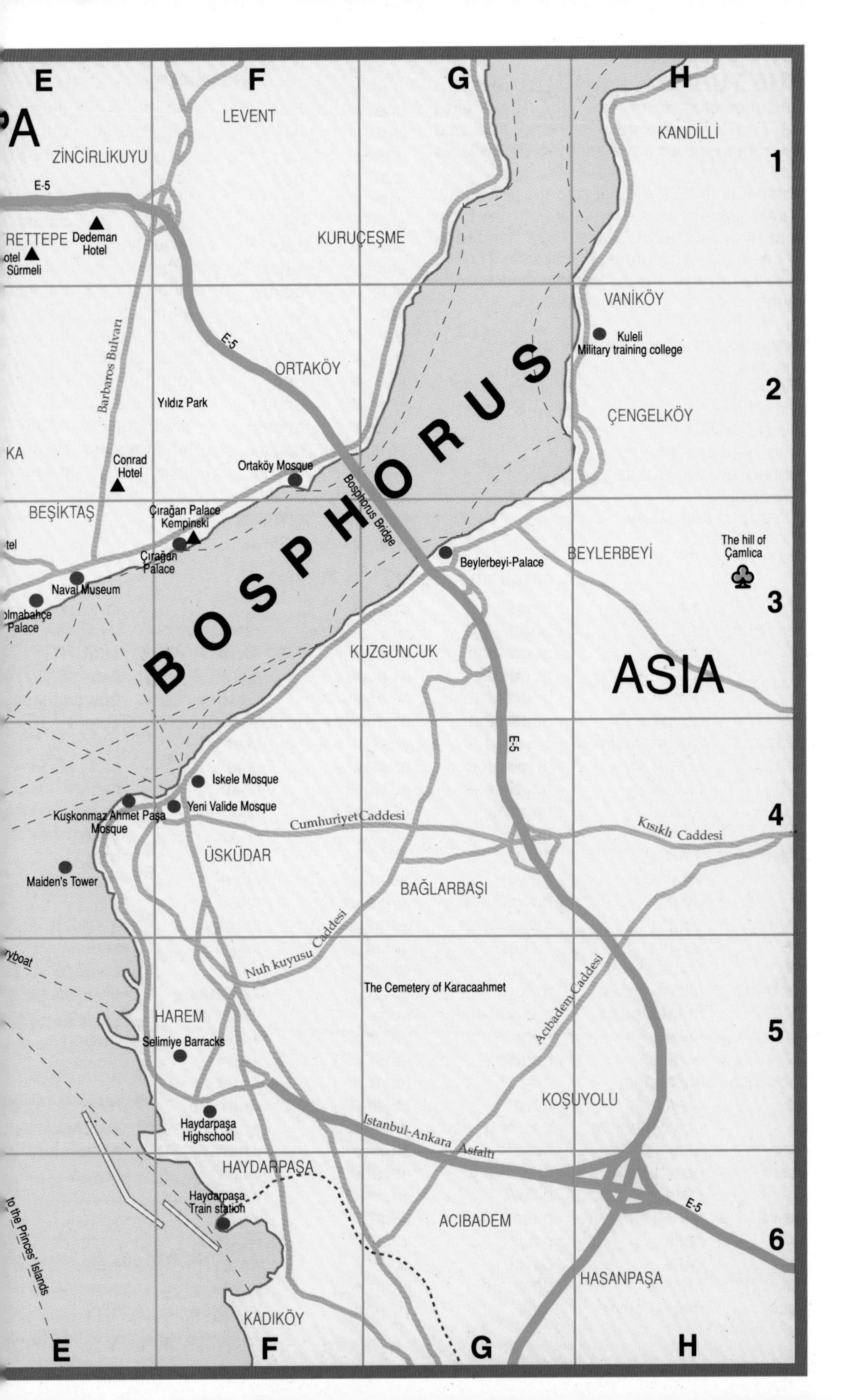

E
F
G
H
PA
LEVENT
KANDİLLİ
ZİNCİRLİKUYU
1
E-5
RETTEPE
Dedeman Hotel
otel Sürmeli
KURUÇEŞME
VANİKÖY
Barbaros Bulvarı
E-5
Kuleli Military training college
ORTAKÖY
BOSPHORUS
2
Yıldız Park
ÇENGELKÖY
KA
Conrad Hotel
Ortaköy Mosque
Bosphorus Bridge
BEŞİKTAŞ
Çırağan Palace Kempinski
tel
Çırağan Palace
Beylerbeyi-Palace
BEYLERBEYİ
The hill of Çamlıca
Naval Museum
3
lmabahçe Palace
KUZGUNCUK
ASIA
E-5
Iskele Mosque
Yeni Valide Mosque
Kuşkonmaz Ahmet Paşa Mosque
Cumhuriyet Caddesi
Kısıklı Caddesi
4
ÜSKÜDAR
Maiden's Tower
BAĞLARBAŞI
ryboat
Nuh kuyusu Caddesi
Acıbadem Caddesi
The Cemetery of Karacaahmet
HAREM
5
Selimiye Barracks
KOŞUYOLU
Haydarpaşa Highschool
Istanbul-Ankara Asfaltı
HAYDARPAŞA
E-5
Haydarpaşa Train station
to the Princes' Islands
ACIBADEM
6
HASANPAŞA
KADIKÖY
E
F
G
H

THE TURKISH LANGUAGE

Turkish originates from the Ural-Altaic languages and is structured like Hungarian and Finnish; root syllables have another root syllable attached to them.
At the same time as the other reforms in Turkey, the Arabic alphabet was replaced by the Latin alphabet (Nov. 1. 1928). Since 1932, language reform has been in progress, introducing Turkish words in lieu of their Arab, Persian and French synonyms.

Pronunciation of a few irregular sounds:

â - as in c**a**r
c - as in **j**ar, **j**ump
ç - as in **ch**apel
e - as in s**e**t, m**e**t
ğ - soft g, between h and g
ı - undotted, between i and g (waited, bitter)
k - as in **c**old, **c**ure
ş - as in **s**ugar, **sh**oe, **sh**ut
y - as in **y**es, **y**ou

Numbers

one	bir	thirty	otuz
two	iki	thirty one	otuz bir
three	üç	thirty two	otuz iki
four	dört	forty	kırk
five	beş	fifty	elli
six	altı	sixty	altmış
seven	yedi	seventy	yetmiş
eight	sekiz	eighty	seksen
nine	dokuz	ninety	doksan
ten	on	hundred	yüz
eleven	onbir	two hundred	iki yüz
twelve	oniki	three hundred	üç yüz
thirteen	onüç	four hundred	dörtyüz
fourteen	ondört	thousand	bin
fifteen	onbeş	two thousand	iki bin
sixteen	onaltı	ten thousand	on bin
seventeen	onyedi	million	milyon
eightteen	onsekiz		
nineteen	ondokuz		
twenty	yirmi		

A small vocabulary in Turkish

airport	hava alanı
aniseed liquor	rakı
a lot	çok
a little	az
beer	bira
big	büyük
bill, account	hesap, fatura
black	siyah, kara
blanket	battaniye
blue	mavi
bread	ekmek
breakfast	kahvaltı
butter	tereyağı
cheap	ucuz
cheers	şerefe
cheese	peynir
chicken	tavuk
clothes brush	elbise fırçası
coat	manto, palto
coffee	kahve
cold	soğuk
dirt-track race	kül tablası
dentist	dişçi
doctor	doktor, hekim
entrance	giriş
excursion	gezi, tur
exit	çıkış
expensive	pahalı
fish	balık
fork	çatal
fruit	meyve
fruit juice	meyve suyu
glass	bardak
good	iyi
good morning	günaydın
good day	iyi günler
good evening	iyi akşamlar
good night	iyi geceler
green	yeşil
greengrocer	manav
hairdresser	kuaför
handbag	el çantası
help!	imdat!
hotel	otel
how?	nasıl?
how much?	kaç para?
information	danışma
jacket	ceket
knife	bıçak
milk	süt
mineral water	soda
near	yakın
neddle	iğne
no	hayır
olive	zeytin
pair of trousers	pantalon
pay	ödeme
pharmacy	eczane
pillow	yastık
plate	tabak
please	lütfen
police	polis
postcard	kartpostal
quilt	yorgan
red	kırmızı
restaurant	lokanta
room	oda
salt	tuz
shaving-soap	traş sabunu
shower	duş
skirt	etek
small	ufak, küçük
soap	sabun
spoon	kaşık
sugar	şeker
suitcase	bavul
table	masa
tea	çay
thanks	teşekkür
token	jeton
toilet	tuvalet
toothpaste	diş macunu
tweezers	cımbız
waiter	garson
warm	sıcak
water	su
welcome!	hoş geldiniz!
what time is it?	saat kaç?
when	ne zaman?
white	beyaz
white cheese	beyaz peynir
why?	neden, niçin?
window	pencere
wine	şarap
yellow	sarı
yesterday	dün

Silhouette of Mosques in the Old City

ISLAM, ITS PRAYERS AND MOSQUES

What does Islam mean and what functions does a mosque have? You'd probably like to know more about them.

As a religion,Islam is a body of doctrines and procedures which were announced by Muhammad and compiled into the Koran. They were spread by Muhammad's actions and persuasion. Islam has over 450 million followers and reaches from Morocco in the West to Pakistan in the East. It's closer to theJewish and Christian faiths than any other religion.

In Islam one believes in the other world and in resurrection. In the Koran (that consists of 114 so-called "Sure" chapters, of 6666 verses each), only two angels are mentioned by name: Gabriel, upon whom Muhammad bestowed his revelations, and Michael, who carried out God's commands on Earth.

Islam recognizes five eminent prophets preceding Muhammad: Adam, Noah, Abraham, Moses and Jesus. Islam doesn't recognize sacraments such as christening or first communion.

Islam is based on five rules which are often referred to as the «Five Commandments of Islam»: faith, prayer, alms, fasting and pilgrimage.

The 1st Commandment is the Faith:

Without doubt you have to believe that there is only one God (Allah) and that Muhammad is His prophet.

The 2nd Commandment is Prayer:

You have to pray five times a day according to the specified method. Before each time of prayer the muezzin calls followers to prayer from the minaret. There is the morning prayer-call (at sunrise), the noon prayer-call, the afternoon call, the evening call (at sunset) and the night prayer-call.

He calls:
God is Almighty
I believe there is no God but Allah
I believe that Muhammad is Allah's prophet
Come to pray
Come to redemption,
God is Almighty
There is no God but Allah.

Prior to every time of prayer, a cleansing ritual is performed, when the face, hands, and arms up to the elbow, the feet and hair are all washed. This act cleanses the body, whereas prayer purifies the soul. The body parts that touch the prayer-rug must be clean.

Moslems can pray wherever they choose, but on Fridays they have to perform the prayer ritual with the community in a mosque. The Friday prayer is the main prayer of the week for Moslems and corresponds to the Sunday morning service of the Christians. Working people who cannot pray at the specific times may make this up later, and the elderly who cannot kneel down may pray sitting.

During the prayer the believer turns to the south-east, the direction of holy Mecca, stands still, bows, kneels down and touches his forehead on the prayer-rug, then he stands up again and repeats the same movements. A prayer takes approximately 10-25 min.

The 3rd Commandment is to give Alms:

Every well-to-do Muslim has to give 2.5% of his yearly income in cash or in goods to the poor, needy widows and orphans. The alms aren't taxes but are contributions in the name of Allah.

The 4th Commandment is to Fast:

Except for children, the sick and travellers, every Muslim is obliged to fast. The month of fasting is called Ramadan, and is the ninth month in the Arab calender. During Ramadan in daylight hours eating, drinking and sexual activity are not allowed. Fasting teaches the Muslim to control his body and to understand the suffering of the poor.

The end of Ramadan is celebrated with a three-day feast called Şeker Bayramı during which people wear new dresses and pay visits to their relatives. Sweets and desserts are served for the occasion. After the morning prayer, families visit the tombs of their loved ones.

The 5th Commandment is to make a Pilgrimage:

Every Muslim who is healthy and has no financial problems is expected to make a pilgrimage to Mecca once in his lifetime. The official pilgrimage takes place two months after Ramadan. The pilgrims have to be dressed identically which reminds people of the fact that everybody is the same in God's presence.

The Mosque:

The style of all the mosques is the same as Muhammad's house in Medina which consisted of cottages around a yard. It was the site of private prayers, a place of political meetings and home of the homeless believers. After Muhammad passed away (632 A.D.), the house became his burial site.

In the 11th century this ancient style evolved into the fundamental mosque model, the so-called open-yard-mosque. Halls surrounded a spacious yard; but this design only suited warm countries whereas the closed mosque was preferred in cold countries.

The domed mosque was improved by the Ottomans. It reached the peak of its popularity during

A praying Muslim

the reign of Sultan Süleyman II (16th century), and we are thankful to his architect Sinan for the most fascinating mosques in Istanbul.

In Istanbul there are two kinds of mosques:

1- Mosques of the sultans

2- Ordinary mosques

The mosques of the sultans are magnificent structures with a lot of minarets, a front yard and an outer yard where sultans and their kinsmen are buried. The outer yard is surrounded by the public buildings of the mosque (a Koran school, a library, a hospital, a public kitchen and a Turkish bath).

The schematic representation of a sultan's mosque

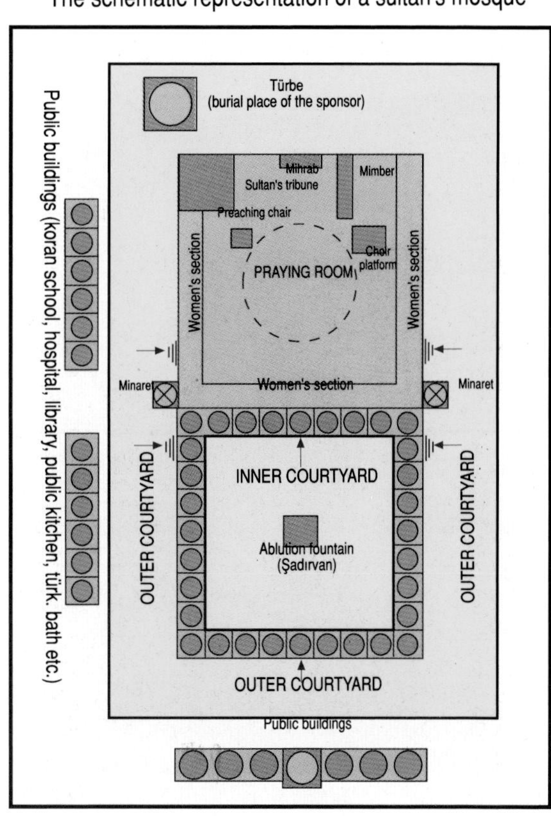

The inner courtyard of a mosque

Mihrab of Rüstempaşa mosque

Ordinary mosques are smaller and usually have one minaret. They consist of a prayer hall and a small front yard or lobby, with the tomb of the sponsor.

What are the important elements of a mosque? In the middle of the south-east wall there is the «mihrab» (prayer niche) where the «imam» leads in prayer five times a day. To the right of the mihrab stands a triangular «mimber» (the Friday pulpit). In the front there is the tribune where the muezzin calls the believers to prayer To the right of this tribune the imam preaches before the Friday prayers. The galleries are reserved for women only.

Mosques of the sultans also have a barred loge for the sultan and his harem to pray.

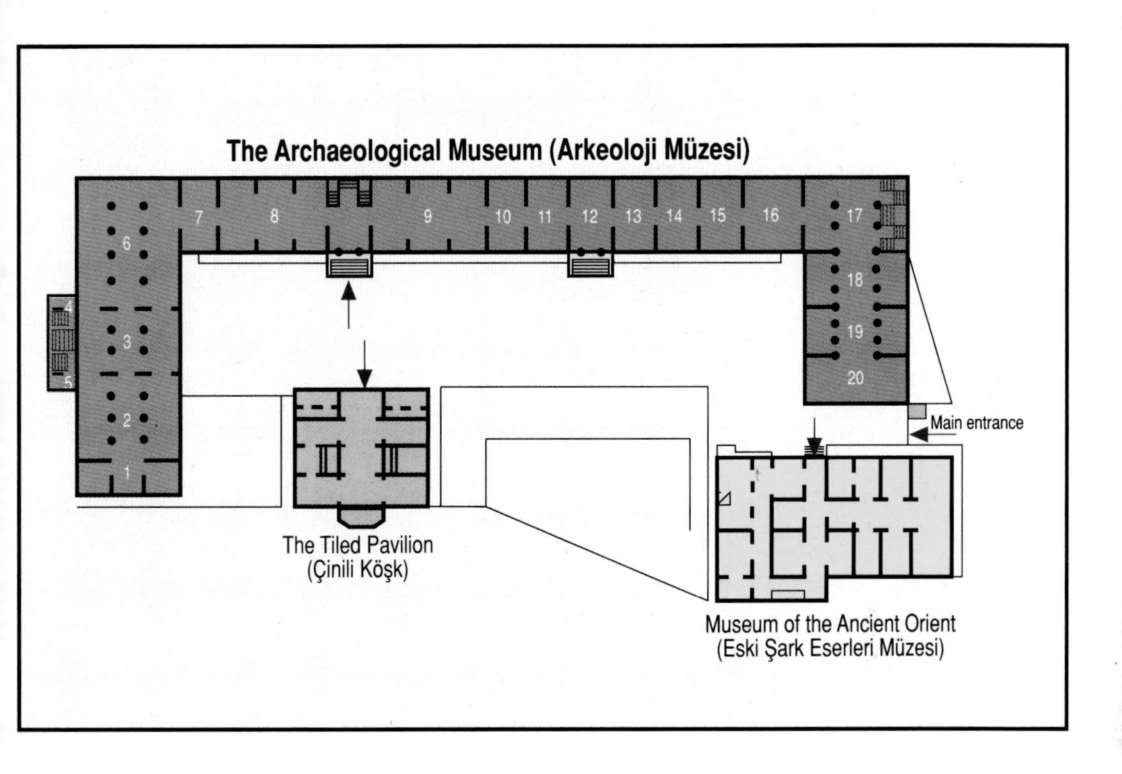

THE OLD CITY

MUSEUMS

The Archaelogical Museum (Arkeoloji Müzesi) D5

This extraordinary museum was established in the reign of Sultan Abdülhamit II by the painter and collector Osman Hamdi Bey. It now houses the best antique collection in the world. The antiquities mostly originate from Anatolia, the Middle East and North Africa, which belonged to the Ottoman Empire. Those who would like to find out more about classical and ancient art should spend a few hours in this interesting museum.

The museum has two floors. The rooms on the ground floor are numbered from 1 to 20, and on the floor above there are halls for sculptures.

ROOM 8:
Turning left at the entrance you come to room 8 where the Sarcophagus of Alexander the Great (4th B.C.) is exhibited; it was discovered at Sidon. It has the form of a Greek temple and is adorned with sculptures; their colours are faded. On the sides, a battle between Greek and Persian armies, and also a lion hunt are depicted. Both representations show Alexander the Great wearing an imperial headband and a lion skin riding his horse.

In addition, battle scenes and a panther hunt are depicted along the narrow sides. The sarcophagus is assumed to belong to one of Alexander's generals.

In this room there are three more sarcophagi

Alexander's Sarcophagus

Alexander's bust

which were discovered at the same site.

At the back there is the sarcophagus of the Mourners (4th B.C.) from Sidon, the sides are composed of 18 columns and depict sitting or standing women in deep grief.

ROOM 7:
(The Sidonian Room)

This contains Roman lead coffins and sarcophagi from the Phoenician harbour Sidon.

ROOM 6:
(The Room of Sepulchral Monuments)

With the exception of the Lycian sarcophagus (No. 343), all the exhibited sarcophagi originate from the Roman Empire. The most interesting sarcophagi are those of Phaedra and Hippolytus (No. 508) and the Meleager Sarcophagus (No. 2100).

ROOMS 4 and 5:

Located on both sides of the staircase, these inaccessible rooms are now used as storage places.

ROOM 3:
(The Sidamara Room)

The main attraction is the magnificent sarcophagus of Sidamara (3rd B.C.), which was discovered in Konya in 1953. On its sides Demeter, Artemis and the sons of Zeus are depicted. Aside from that representation, we see a hunting scene, athletes and a chariot race. Depicted on the lid are the dead man and his wife.

In addition, smaller sarcophagi discovered in Sidamara are exhibited in this room.

ROOM 2:
(Architectural finds)

Interesting mosaics from the 5th century B.C. and a lot of items from the Hellenistic era are displayed in the room. On the right wall we see fragments from the frieze of the temple of Artemis Leucophriene at Magnesia on the Meander (2nd B.C.). On the left wall are the fragments from the frieze of the temple of Hecate at Lagina. On the friezes, combats between Greeks and Amazons are represented. (2nd. B.C.)

ROOM 1:
(Room of Epigraphs)

Once this room was used as a storage place, but now funerary stele and inscriptions of the Hellenistic and Roman eras are exhibited.
To the right of the entrance lobby is

ROOM 9:
(Tabnit Room)

It's important to mention these three magnificent sarcophagi:

The Satrap Sarcophagus (5th B.C.): The oldest sarcophagus from the necropolis of Sidon shows the satrap, i.e. the governor, of a Persian province on the throne, hunting, and at a feast with his servants.

The Lycian Sarcophagus (5th B.C.): It's from the necropolis of Sidon. Its high roof is typically Lycian (i.e.of south-west Asia Minor). The figures in relief, of two beautiful sphinxes and a battle scene involving two bearded centaurs (creatures with a man's head and a horse's body) are depicted.
The Tabnit Sarcophagus (6th B.C.): This sarcophagus held the remains of Tabnit, father of Eshmounazar II, whose mummy is now exposed in a case beneath the window.

ROOM 10:
(The Phoenician Room)

A lot of sarcophagi in the form of human bodies from the 4th and 5th B.C. are exhibited. Phoenician inscriptions decorate the walls.

ROOM 11:
(The Archaic Room)

Funerary stele, archaic reliefs, the relief with Heraclius on his knees, and a high Phoenician stele representing a chariot are exhibited in this room.

ROOM 12:
(The Assos Room)

Fragments of the frieze from the temple of Assos, the only Doric temple in Anatolia, and a colossal statue of Bes,the Cypriot Hercules,holding up a headless lioness by her hind paws are exhibited.

ROOM 13:
(The Athenian Room)

The most noteworthy exhibit is the replica of the statue of Hermes by Alcamenes, the student of Phidias. There is also a fine statue of Athena, a lioness (4th B.C.) from the mausoleum at Halicarnassus (Bodrum), one of the seven wonders of the ancient world, the torso of Asklepios and the welfare god, from the island of Kos.

ROOM 14:
(The Philiscos Room)

ra-Sarcophagus

Sarcophagus of the Mourners

The Ephebos Youth

This room houses statues of the Muses and the Apollo Citharados (2th A.D.). also the statue of Are, the daughter of Neon, which is the unique and original work of the famous Philiscos of Rhodes.

ROOM 15:
(The Ephebos Room)

In the middle is the most impressive work in the room. It's the statue of Ephebos of Tralles, which represents a youth resting after exercising; he is standing in a relaxed attitude with a cape draped round him to protect him from the cold. To the right of Ephebos is the bust of Alexander the Great, a copy of the original by Lyssipus, and a colossal statue of Apollo of Tralles from the 3rd century.

ROOM 16:
(The Attis Room)

Here we see the statue of Attis, the Phrygian god of fertility, the statuette of Hygiea, goddess of health and the statue of Zeus of Pergamon.

ROOM 17:
(The Aphrodisias Room)

In the middle of the room stands the statue of the river-god Neptune (2nd A.D.) from the Vedius Gymnasium in Ephesus. Against the left wall is a statue of Tyche, the goddess of fortune from the Roman era and the statue of Dionysus of Synnada.

ROOM 18:
(The Roman Room)

On the right side are the busts of the Roman emperors e.g. Augustus, Tiberius, Marc Aurelius. On the left side we see the statues of Zeus, Athena and Emperor Hadrian.

ROOM 19:
(Room of Christian Art)

This room contains antiquities from Byzantine Constantinople as well as from the medieval Genoese town in Istanbul The gravestones of the Latin families from the church of Saint Paul in Galata are very interesting (today's Arab Mosque).

ROOM 20:
(The Byzantine Room)

This is the last room on the ground floor and is devoted to Byzantine antiquities unearthed in Istanbul. On the mosaic pavement we see Orpheus with animals, and there are two marble pedestals standing to either side of the pavement. The pedestals, which once bore a bronze statue of Porphyrios, the famous charioteer, commemorate his victories in the Hippodrome.

THE SECOND FLOOR

Sixteen rooms contain smaller finds such as jewellery,ceramics, bronze items, glasses and coins. The gold jewels are prehistoric. The ivory inlay of Eudokia, the wife of Theodosius II, is noteworthy. Besides that, it's worth mentioning the serpent head from the tripod in the Hippodrome, a fragment of a Herakles statue and the statuette of Herakles carrying a club which is an important bronze find.

A ceramic panel which decorated the holy road at Ishtar Gate in Babylon

Museum of the Ancient Orient (Eski Şark Eserleri Müzesi) D5

The Museum of the Ancient Orient is a part of the adjacent Archaeological Museum. The building which was once an art academy, was built in 1883. After reconstruction and reorganization, the museum was opened in 1974. The exhibits are displayed in nine rooms.

Room 1: **Findings from the Arabian Peninsu-** (pre-Islamic period) (window 1) **la**

Funerary stele, figures and statues of sandstone are exhibited.

Room 2: **Findings from Ancient Egypt** (windows 2 and 3)

The granite sphinxes, mummy cases, statuettes and belongings found in the graves are noteworthy.

Room 3: **Findings from Mesopotamia** (windows 4-8)

a) Halaf-Culture (5th B.C.)

b) Ninive-Culture (3rd B.C.) (Ninive was the capital of Assyria and was destroyed by the Babylonians in the 7th century.)

c) Ancient Sumerian culture (3rd-4th B.C.)

Room 4: **Findings from Akkad** (window 8)

Important are the clay tiles with printed characters. These are the oldest printed letters yet discovered. (3rd B.C.)

Findings from the Early Summerian Era (window 9)

Stone statues and the representation of Mesopotamian cosmology are interesting (3rd c.B.C.)

Findings from the Ancient Babylonian Era (window 10)

Here we see two diorite statues: On the left side is the statue of Tura Dagan and on the right side the one of his son Ishtar, the head of which, is a copy of the original in the East Berlin museum (3rd B.C.).

Findings from the Early-and Mid-Assyrian Period (windows 11 and 12)

Two panels of lead 350 kg each, and inscriptions of the Ishtar Temple are displayed. In the centre is the basalt statue of King Salmanasar (8th B.C.). In window 12, the bronze facing of

The basalt statue of King Salmanasar

the temple Maru is exhibited.

Room 5: **Findings of the Early Assyrian Period**

An obelisk with cunei-form characters stands in the centre. Besides that, small findings of clay (window 13), clay panels with cuneiform (window 14) and the code by Hammurabi, the oldest code in the world, are displayed.

Room 6: **Findings of the Urartu Period**

Here are round or flat Mesopotamian seals of ivory, metal, clay and wood (window 16), small findings dating back from the early Babylonian period (window 17) and findings from Asia Minor (window 18)

Room 7: **Foundations of the Hittite culture**

We see one of the four sphinxes from the Hittite capital «Hattusha» (Bogazköy) on the left side of the room. The main attraction of the museum is the famous treaty «Kadesh» written in Hittite cuneiform on clay panels and signed by Ramses II and Hattusilas. It was discovered in Bogazköy in 1960. (window 20)

Room 8: **Findings of the Hittite and Ancient Anatolian Period**

The basalt sphinxes, the torso of a Hittite king "Halparunda II", and the lions of basalt are admirable.

Room 9: **Various findings**

Among other items a funerary stele with a Hittite relief and a relief of the Hittite god «Teschup» with a hieroglyphic inscription (9th B.C.) are important.

An Assyrian basalt panel

The Tiled Pavilion "Çinili Köşk"

The Tiled Pavilion (Çinili Köşk) D5

In 1472 Sultan Mehmet II (the Conqueror) had «Çinili Köşk» built as a pleasure pavilion outside the palace. Once it was covered with mosaics and blue-green tiles; this is how its name originated. The design and decorations are of Persian influence. The pavilion consists of two perpendicular storeys

A ceramic tile from Iznik

All the rooms were tiled previously.

Room 1: (To the left of the entrance) has a small collection of Selçuk tiles and ceramics (12th-14th c.)

Room 2: (On the ieft) has a nice collection of tiles from the Selçuk and Ottoman Periods (14th-15th centuries)

The Central Room: Contains the superb mihrab from the mosque of Ibrahim Bey at Karaman (Iznik tiles) and two pretty lunette panels from the mosque of Haseki Hürrem in Istanbul. (14th-15th c.)

Rooms 3 and 4: They contain precious Iznik tiles from the 16th and 17th centuries. The attractive baroque fountain, partly tiled and partly painted, is placed in a niche in the wall.

Rooms 5 and 6: These last rooms house 18th and 19th century ceramics influenced by European taste.

When you leave the Tiled Pavilion, you have the Archaeological Museum with the mighty Byzantine sarcophagus (5th and 6th A.D.) in front of you. To your right there is a tea garden between the antique fragments where you can rest after your tour.

Gate of Peace Salutations "Bab-üs-Selam"

Topkapı Palace (Topkapı Sarayı) D5

Topkapı Palace is the most extensive monument in Turkish çivil architecture. The monument occupies 700,000 square metres, and is a building complex of courts, pavilions, mosques and fountains. Its name «Topkapı» is a compound and means «Cannon Gate». The palace is surrounded by a wall extending from the Byzantine seawalls along the Golden Horn to those along the Marmara Sea.

When Mehmet II conquered Istanbul in 1453, he had his first palace erected in the district where the University of Istanbul and Süleymaniye Mosque are now situated. Since the palace was fairly small, in 1459 he decided to build Topkapı Palace. Only the harem was added later in the 16th century. The palace was the official residence of the sultans until 1839 when Sultan Abdülmecit I moved to the new palace, «Dolmabahçe», (see page 92).

In the golden ages of the empire approx. 4000 people lived in this palace district. The total area included four grand courts and the harem section.

TOPKAPI PALACE

1. Gate of Salutations (Bab-üs-Selam Kapısı)
2. The Old Kitchen (Collection of Chinese and Japanese Porcelain)
3. The Old Olive-Oil Refinery and Soap Factory (Collection of Glass and Porcelain Items (manifactured in Istanbul)
4. Collection of European Porcelain and Silverware
5. Gate of Felicity (Bab-üs-Saadet)
6. Meeting Hall of the Privy Council (Kubbealtı)
7. Collection of Arms
8. The Royal Stables (Collection of the Royal Carriages)
9. The Imperial Hall (Arz Odası)
10. The Apartments of the White Eunuchs (Collection of Embroidery)
11. School of Expedition for Page Boys (Collection of Royal Gowns)
12. Treasury
13. Gallery of Portraits and Miniatures
14. Collection of Clocks
15. Collection of Relics
16. Calligraphy Collection
17. The New Library
18. Library of Sultan Ahmet III
19. "Sofa" Mosque
20. Tower of the Head Physician
21. Terrace Pavilion
22. Baghdad Pavilion
23. Revan Pavilion
24. Pavilion of Sultan İbrahim (Circumcision Room of the Princes)
25. Mecidiye Pavilion (the fine "Konyalı Restaurant")

HAREM

1. The Carriage Gate (Arabalar Kapısı)
2. Guard Room of the Black Eunuchs
3. Black Eunuchs' Mosque
4. Yard of the Black Eunuchs
5. Apartments of the Black Eunuchs
6. Rooms of the Black Eunuchs
7. School of the Princes
8. The Main Gate (Cümle Kapısı)
9. Courtyard of the "Cariyeler" (Cariyeler Taşlığı)
10. The Room with a Hearth (Ocaklı Sofa)
11. Apartments of the Sultan's Mother
12. Bathroom of the Sultan's Mother
13. Bathroom of the Sultan
14. Bedroom of Sultan Abdülhamit I
15. Suite of Sultan Selim III
16. Terrace with Pool
17. Pavilion of Osman III
18. The Feast or Throne Hall (Hünkar Sofası)
19. Hall of Murat III
20. Library of Ahmet I
21. The Fruit Room of Sultan Ahmet III
22. Apartments of the Princes
23. Sitting Rooms of the "Haseki"
24. Courtyard of the Favourites
25. Apartment of Abdülhamit I
26. The Golden Road
27. The Birdcage Gate

TOPKAPI PALACE MUSEUM

FOURTH COURT

Restaurant
Café

THIRD COURT

Exit of the harem

Entrance
of the harem

SECOND COURT

FIRST COURT

Harem

Vase of green celadon-Chinese

Vase of blue-white porcelain-Chinese

The First Court

The main entrance to the Palace is through Bab-ı Humayun (the Imperial Gate), the first palace gate (built in 1428). The first court is being used as a parking lot today; to the left you see Haghia Eirene.

The Second Court

Through the second gate called Bab-üs-Selam (Gate of Salutations) (No. 1 on the key) you reach the second court. Here there are six paths:

To the right, the first and second paths lead to the Palace Kitchen(No.2)The third path goes to the third gate «Bab-üs-Saadet» (No.5)The fourth one takes you to the Divan (Council Chamber) (No.6) The fifth path leads to the Harem.

The left-hand path, the sixth one, goes to the Privy Stables. (No.8).

We take the second path and come to the **Palace Kitchen;** after a fire it was reconstructed by Sinan in 1574. It's a long building of ten rooms with domes and chimneys. For over three hundred years, 800 men at a time worked here as kitchen staff. This number went up to 1000 at feasts. The yearly meat supply of this oversized kitchen included 30.000 chickens, 23.000 sheep, 14.000 calves and large amounts of fruit and vegetables.

Today, the kitchen houses the display of the rich collection of Chinese and Japanese porcelain. After those at Peking and Dresden it is said to be the third richest collection in the world with 10.700 rare and valuable pieces.

The rooms are arranged as follows:

Celadon Series (10th-14th c.)

These are the oldest and most valuable pieces of porcelain in the whole collection. Celadon is actually a mixture of jade and caolin. When poisonous food is served, celadon changes its colour and the enamel splits, which is an interesting feature, since the sultans were scared of being poisoned. The items belong to the Ming, Yuan and Sung dynasties.

Blue- White Series (14th-19th c.)

These account for the largest part of the collection and come from the Ming Dynasty. The white background is decorated with landscape, dragon, animal and flower motives in cobalt-blue.

The Single Coloured Series (15th-17th c.)

These are the white and yellow porcelain items from the Ming era.

The Colourful Series (16th-18th c.)

These are items chiefly from the late Ming Dynasty.

Collection of Japanese Porcelains (17th-19th c.)

They make up only a small portion of the collection. In general they are very colourful, and were manufactured according to European taste as export items.

The antique bronze and copper utensils of the court kitchen are displayed in one of the adjacent rooms Here you see cauldrons and pots of prodigious size, gold-plated kettles, jars etc.

The small building with domes at the north end of the kitchen served as an olive-oil refinery and factory for soap manufacture. Now it houses a lovely porcelain and glass collection made by Istanbul manufacturers of the eighteenth and nineteenth centuries. (No.3)

Collection of European Porcelain and Silverware (No.4)

This collection is displayed opposite the kitchen and has been exhibited on two floors since 1984. In the basement there are fascinating silver items, mainly gifts presented to the sultans, whereas you see only European porcelain on the upper floor. (Limoges, Sevres, Meissen, Augarten, Petersburg etc.) (18th-19th c.)

Divan-Tower "Kubbealtı"

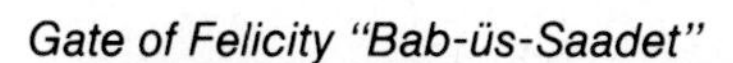

Gate of Felicity "Bab-üs-Saadet"

We now proceed to the **Divan** or **Council Chamber (Kubbealtı)** (No. 6)

The Divan consists of two adjacent rooms:

a) The Office of the Grand Vizier

b) The Public Records Office.

Over the Grand Vizier's seat there is a window grill. When the Council was in session the Sultan could overhear the proceedings unseen behind it. During those sessions the district was controlled from the huge tower to prevent any kind of espionage. In this room the Vizier also received foreign ambassadors.

Collection of Arms (No.7)

The building with heavily barred windows located next to the Divan is one of the oldest units of the palace. The Sultan's treasure used to be stored here, and today, Turkish, Arabic and Persian armour are displayed in it.

The fifth path leads to the Harem.

Following the sixth path you come to the **Sultan's stables** (No.8) where valuable imperial carriages and harnesses are now displayed.

The third middle path leads us to a gate with a roof in the front which is supported by four columns:

"**Bab-üs-Saadet**" Gate (Gate of Felicity) of the sixteenth century. (No. 5) In front of this gate, the new Sultan's accession to the throne, the receiving of homage on religious holidays, and the bestowing of titles upon the army commanders took place.

The Third Court

Behind the Gate of Felicity stands the **Arz Odası** (Audience Room) (No.9) In this elaborately decorated building, the Sultan sitting on his gold and emerald throne received ambassadors from foreign countries. During these sessions, water running from the fountain built at the entrance of the building, prevented people from listening to the confidential discussions. To both sides of the Gate of Felicity were the quarters of the White Eunuchs who were in charge of the administration and discipline of the School (No.10). In the rooms that take up the eastern side of the court, the collection of embroidery there can be examined.

To the east the court includes the Seferli Koğuşu (School of Expedition pages) (No.11), which consists of two long adjacent rooms and now houses the **Imperial Wardrobe.** In the front room, a fascinating collection of costumes worn by the sultans and made of silk, satin or velvet brocade is on display. The costumes of the princes,

Audience Hall

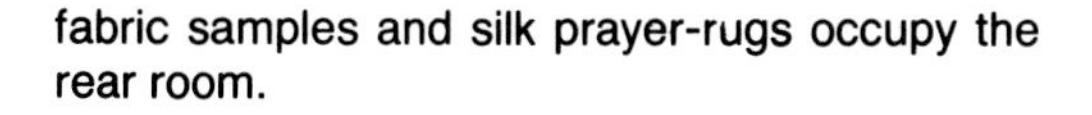

World-famous dagger

"Spoonmaker's Diamond

fabric samples and silk prayer-rugs occupy the rear room.

The Treasury: (No.12)

This building was built as a summer palace for Mehmet II., and in the sixteenth century it was converted into a treasury during the reign of Selim I. Today very precious and unique pieces of jewellery which belonged to the sultans are displayed in four rooms. Some of the pieces were gifts, some were bought by the sultans and some were tributes.

Room 1:

In the middle are gold be-jewelled swords and daggers, crystal waterpipes, coffee cups and valuable bowls. Among these items the statuettes of a black slave and a sheik sitting on the throne deserve special attention,because the legs of the slave and the body of the sheik are each made from a big pearl.

In the showcases you see the gorgeous armour of Sultan Mustafa III, the throne of Murat IV decorated with ivory and mother-of-pearl, water pitchers, jars, golden candlesticks, a cane with a diamond grip (given to Sultan Abdülhamit.II by the German Emperor Wilhelm II),the golden model of a Chinese palace and an Indian golden music box with a golden elephant motive (17 th century).

Room 2:

In the middle stands the throne of Sultan Ahmet I (17th c.) made of walnut wood Around you are precious pendants, the magnificent pendulum of Abdülhamit I. and Ahmet I.,a jewelled turban, a tuft of feathers decorated with diamonds and rubies, objects of jade, a golden cradle for the new-born princes, and behind the throne of Ahmet I hangs the world-famous dagger from the movie «Topkapı»; the golden grip is studded with three big emeralds. In the same showcase one emerald weighs 3 260 grams (the biggest emerald in the world), the other one's weight amounts to 1 310 grams.

Room 3:

This room houses the seventh biggest diamond in the world, the Spoonmaker's Diamond. It's 86 carats and is mounted in silver and surrounded by 49 brilliants.

In the 18th century, a French official called Pigot bought this diamond from a maharajah and brought it to France. Napoleon's mother bought it in an auction. However, she sold her jewellery to rescue her son from exile. Tepedelenli Ali Paşa (Grand Vizier) purchased it. Since he co-operated in a rebellion against Sultan Mahmut II in the 19th century, his treasure and property were confiscated. That's the story of how the diamond came to

Jewelled jar

Golden compote set decorated with brilliants

the palace. The evidence for this legend is a picture of Ali Paşa with a very similar diamond on his turban. Besides the diamond two golden chandeliers, each weighing 48 kg and studded with 6666 brilliants, are displayed in this room. The gold 250 kg «Bayram-throne»(used on religious holidays), is encrusted with precious stones, the rose-water spray, the jewelled Koran covers, incense jars Between the third and the fourth room is a terrace with an impressive view. Don't miss it!

Room 4:

In the middle of this room, stands the gold Turkish-Indian throne encrusted with pearls and emeralds, a gift to Sultan Mahmut I from the Persian Shah Nadir.

In the showcases the hand and arm bones mounted in gold of John the Baptist, valuable snuff-boxes, latches of ivory, splendid spoons and guns etc. are on display.

Pavilion of Portraits and Miniatures (No.13)

This is a building with lofted floors. On the first floor, miniatures, calligraphies and paintings from the Turkish-Islamic world (13th-17th c.) are exhibited. In the mezzanine there is a collection of portraits of the sultans. The building was named « Kiler Koğuşu»(School of Commissariat pages).

Collection of Clocks(No.14)

The collection consists of fabulous Turkish, English and French clocks from the 16th-20th

"Bayram" throne

The Turkish-Indian throne

centuries. The two cages, clocks at the same time, and a French astronomy device with a built-in clock, are of special attraction.

Collection of Relics (No.15)

The building which has a facade embellished with tiles is the most venerable in the whole complex. In the front hang two big crystal chandeliers in the form of the globe. In the domed rooms, holy Islamic relics and personal relics of the Prophet Muhammad are displayed. They were brought from Egypt by Selim I after his conquest of that country in 1517. The walls are covered with the most superb tiles from Iznik.

In the first room are the swords of the first four Caliphs, part of the Kaaba Gate at Mecca, its silver-gilt keys, water-gutters from Kaaba and a model of the Umar Mosque in Jerusalem made of mother-of-pearl. This was sent to Sultan Abdülhamit II by the patriarch of Jerusalem, to commemorate his 25th anniversary on the throne (19th century).

In the second room in a small showcase, the solid gold covering for the Hacer-i Esved, the holy stone from Kaaba is displayed. In another showcase the personal relics of the Prophet are exhibited: His footprint, his seal of amber, one of his ol-

Turkish miniature-16th century

dest letters written on gazelle skin and a box in which hairs from his beard and soil from his burial site are kept.

Through a grill door in the third room one sees the silver throne of the Prophet, which Murat IV had made in the palace in the 17th century. Besides that, the bow and the golden sword of the Prophet are displayed here.

The Sultan used to visit this holy room with his high officials once a year on the 15th day of Ramadan.

Calligraphy Collection (No.16)

This building served as the Hall of the Privy Chamber (Hasoda Koğuşu). It was the highest of the vocational divisions of the Palace School. In the building books, manuscripts and admirable calligraphy are displayed today.

The New Library (No.17)

Dating originally from the 15th century, this is one of the oldest buildings in the palace area, and is called 'Ağalar Camii' (the principal mosque of the Palace School). After the declaration of the Republic it was changed into a library in 1928. Today 13.500 Turkish, Arabic, Persian and Greek books and manuscripts are p eserved here.

Library of Sultan Ahmet III (No.18)

Sultan Ahmet III had his library built in 1719. It's a domed marble building decorated with Iznik tiles. The recess opposite the entrance was the Sultan's reading corner. The ancient inventory book, date of foundation and the axe with which the Sultan made the first blow to the ground, are displayed here. A pretty fountain in the hall embellishes the old library.

The Fourth Court

To the right is the small **«Sofa Mosque»** (No. 19) built by Mahmut II. Farther on is the **«Mecidiye Kiosk»** (No.25), the latest addition to the buildings of the Palace. This was constructed in 1840 by Abdulmecit I before he moved to Dolmabahçe Palace. It displays Turkish architecture under European influence. On its lower floor there is an excellent restaurant overlooking the Marmara Sea.

In the middle of the courtyard stands the "**Hekimbaşı Odası**" (the Chamber of the Head Physician), from the 15th century (No. 20). It had a pharmacy where medicine for the residents of the palace could be ordered. The head physician supervised the preparation of the medicines.

Fountain in front of the library of Ahmet III

Turkish miniature from the 16th century

Islamic relics

The Baghdad Pavilion

The Revan Pavilion with fountain

Mecidiye Pavilion

A baldachino with a gilt-bronze canopy of Sultan Ibrahim

After passing by that tower you come to the «**Sofa Kiosk**» (pavilion with a terrace) (No.21) which is a typical example of Turkish architecture. It was built by Ahmet III. First it served as a recess, and later during the Tulip Epoch (1718-1730), as a lodge for guests. Its garden was the site of the famous tulip festivals celebrated in April every year.

Finally we come to a terrace with an impressive view of the Golden Horn. In the centre of the terrace a balcony with a golden baldachino attracts us. This is where Sultan İbrahim (1640-1648) had his evening meal after sunset in the holy month of Ramadan.

Beyond it stands the "**Bağdad Köşk**" (Baghdad Pavilion) (No. 22) built by Murat IV in 1639 to commemorate his capture of Baghdad. The staircase beside the pavilion leads you to the "**Revan Köşk**" (Revan Pavilion) (No. 23) which was constructed by the same sultan. Both of them are sheathed in tiles within and without, and surrounded by a columned portico.

The last building on the left side of the baldachino is the **pavilion of Sultan İbrahim** (No. 24) of the 17th century. It served as the Circumcision Room of the young princes. Circumcision (see page 86).

The reception room (Harem)

The Harem

The public entrance to the Harem is through the **Carriage Gate** in the second court (No.1). At this gate the ladies of the harem got into their carriages to go to the city.

The word " harem" is Arabic. The Turks use the word "Darüssade" (House of Felicity).Polygamy was first known amongst the Assyrians, later Muslims adopted it and one could marry four wives at the same time. Before Islam the Turkish people were monogamous. In the 10th century, the Turks accepted Islam and also adopted the Arabic harem tradition, which became very popular during the Ottoman Dynasty until Atatürk banned this pratice in 1926.

Since the sultans hardly had time for their private lives because of their battles, the harem wasn't large until the reign of Sultan Süleyman I in the 16th century. The religion allowed men to marry four wives. This law was a result of the wars; many widows had to be provided for, and the army needed new recruits.

The harem ladies lived in the old palace «Çinili Köşk» (see page 22) till the 16th century. Topkapı Palace was an office building for the public business of the Empire. Roxelane , the Russian wife of Süleyman the Magnificent, persuaded him to allow her to live in the new palace with her harem slaves and the eunuchs. Later in the reigns of Selim II and Murat III, additions like the bedrooms of the sultans and their mothers were made, and the harem became a big building complex with 400 rooms. Beginning at the end of the 16th century the entire harem of the sultans lived here.

Today a small part of the harem can be visited; however, I'd like to talk about the important but inaccessible sections as well.

Through the **Carriage Gate** (No. 1) we enter the **Guard Room of the Black Eunuchs** (No. 2) which is revetted with fine tiles. On the left, a door gives access to the **Mosque of the Black Eunuchs** which is also revetted with tiles. (No. 3).

Through another door we enter the **Courtyard of the Black Eunuchs** (No. 4). The **Living Quarters of the Black Eunuchs** (No. 5) are arranged around an inner covered courtyard in three storeys with a tall fire place at one end. There are ten or twelve little rooms on each floor, those on the lower floor belonged to the elderly eunuchs.

On the left side of the courtyard are* **the apartments of the Chief Black Eunuch (Kızlar Ağası)** (No.6), the most powerful official in the Harem, who was mainly responsible for discipline. In official protocol, his position was the fourth place following the sultan, the grand vizier and the "Sheik ül Islam" (the highest religious official). He had close relations with the sultan, the vizier and the mother of the sultan.These relationships gave him the opportunity to get involved in intrigues. Since he was neither a real woman nor a real man, filled with hatred, he would often act against both sexes.

Again starting from the courtyard we pass on the left a staircase that leads up to **the Princes' Schoolrooms** (No.7). These are pretty rooms with valuable tiles from the 17th and 18th centuries. At the end of the open courtyard **the Main Gate (Cümle Kapısı)** (No.8) leads into the Harem. The first room behind the gate is the guardroom from the left side of which a long narrow corridor stretches to the open **Courtyard of the Cariyeler** (women slaves) **(Cariyeler Taşlığı)** (No.9). Along the corridor there are a lot of niches where food served from the kitchen was kept warm.

The «cariye» was a slave bought to serve the sultan or sent to him as a gift. Among them, the ones the sultan liked were called concubines who were given the name "İkbal" (favourite). Each concubine had her own apartment, slaves and eunuchs. Those favourites who became the official wife of the sultan were called "Kadın Efendi" (Sultan's wife). The first one who gave the sultan a son became the first lady. When the sultan especially loved one of the wives, she was called «Haseki» (the loved favourite). In history a few of these favourites are very famous. Although the son

*** Inaccessible rooms**

The Hall of Murat III (Harem)

Fountain in the Hall of Murat III (Harem)

of the first lady should succeed the sultan, those favourites ruled the country.

Crossing the courtyard to the north side we enter a room called **the Room with a Hearth (Ocaklı Oda)** (No.10) a beautiful tiled chamber dominated by a huge bronze chimney piece from which glowing charcoal was carried into the harem. Then we come to **the Courtyard of the Sultan's Mother** (No.11), one of the most important sections of the harem. The mother was the most dominant power in the harem. Her apartments include 40 rooms. The dining-room and the reception hall are open to the public. In the small room to the rear is her elevated bed with a prayer recess next to it.

A short passage leads to the baths. The first one belongs to **the Sultan's mother** (No. 12), and the adjacent one belongs to the Sultan (No. 13). This beautiful bathing area divides into a lounge, a massage room, a dressing-room and the actual bathing area itself of white marbel. The grill was intended to protect the Sultan from a possible assassination attempt.

Opposite the baths is ***the Bedroom of Sultan Abdülhamit I** of the 18th century (No.14). The inner rooms have gilt-bronze rococo paintings, a baldachino bed, and the fountain is embellished with tiles from Vienna.

On the upper floor is ***the Suite of Sultan Selim III** (No.15) from the end of the 18th century, and with a small mosque. From here we enter a terrace* with a pool in the middle, (No.16) and **the pavilion* of Osman III** (No. 17) from the middle of the 18th century, which was renovated in European style at the beginning of the 19th century.

Continuing our walk in the passage to the baths we come to **the Hall of the Emperor (Hünkar Sofası)**(No.18); dating from the late 16th century it is the larges: and grandest room in the Palace. During the reign of Sultan Osman III it was restored in rococo style. In this hall the sultan entertained his close friends. Only his mother, the first lady, the favourites and the cildren were admitted to the hall.The bluish-white tiles on the walls were brought from Holland in the 19th century, the mirrors are of Venetian crystal, the gilt sofa was sent by Kaiser Wilhelm II, and the grandfather clock was a gift from the English Queen Victoria. Through a hidden door, (the mirror cabinet) the sultan could pass into another room in case of an emergency.

The adjacent hall belongs to **Murat III,** (No.19) and was **his bedroom.** This is one of the oldest rooms in the harem and doubtless one of the most beautiful in the Palace, because it retains the whole of its original decoration. It is dated by an inscription to the 16th century and is worthy of Si-

*** Inaccessible rooms**

The Fruit Room of Sultan Ahmet III (Harem)

nan. The walls of the domed room are sheathed in blue and red Iznik tiles. Opposite the fireplace is an elaborate fountain of carved polychrome marble. The fountain prevents outsiders from overhearing conversations, and the rushing of the running water gives the room a cool atmosphere. The bed baldachinos in the corners both belong to the 18th century.

Next to the pavilion of Murat III there are two small rooms. The first one is the small **library of Ahmet I** (No. 20), a small but pretty room. The walls and dome are decorated with İznik tiles. The cabinet doors, shutters and the Koran cover have fine inlaid work of mother-of-pearl and ivory.

The second room is **the Fruit Room (Yemiş Odası) of Sultan Ahmet III** (No.21) with painted panels of fruit. This belongs to the high Tulip Period (1718-1730) and shows the first beginnings of European rococo influence.

Retracing our steps through Murat's Hall we come to a pair of very beautiful rooms where the crown princes had to live in confinement. (No.22). It's believed that the rooms date from the 17th century. They have elaborate windows and valuable tiles, and the wonderful brass-gilt fireplace in the second room is of great attraction.

After leaving the apartments of the crown princes we come to **the sitting-rooms of the "Hasekis"** (No.23) and on the left is **the Hall of the Favourites** (No.24). In the courtyard we see a building built of wood which houses the living-rooms of the favourites and the small **apartment of Abdülhamit I.** (18th c.) (No.25)

Now we're almost at the end of our tour of the harem. A 46m-long, dark passage called the famous **Golden Road (Altın Yol)** (No.26) leads us to the exit. On holidays and accessions the sultans used tu disperse gold coins on this road.

At the end of the Golden Road we turn left and leave the harem through **the Birdcage Gate** (No. 27) **(Kuşhane Kapısı)** where the meals were once brought to the harem.

Haghia Sophia

Museum of Haghia Sophia (Ayasofya Müzesi) D5

Until the conquest of Istanbul by the Turks this great Byzantine building was known to be the centre of religious life in the Byzantine Empire. After the conquest it served as a mosque for nearly 500 years. Since 1935 -thanks to Atatürk- Haghia Sophia has been one of the most popular museums in the world.

Haghia Sophia means "Divine Wisdom". According to a legend: In the year 325, Constantine erected the first basilica which was devasted by a fire in the year 404. In 415, Theodosius II reconstructed the church, but it was burned down during the Nika Revolt in 532. Forty days later Justinian I set out to rebuild the church; the famous architects Anthem-

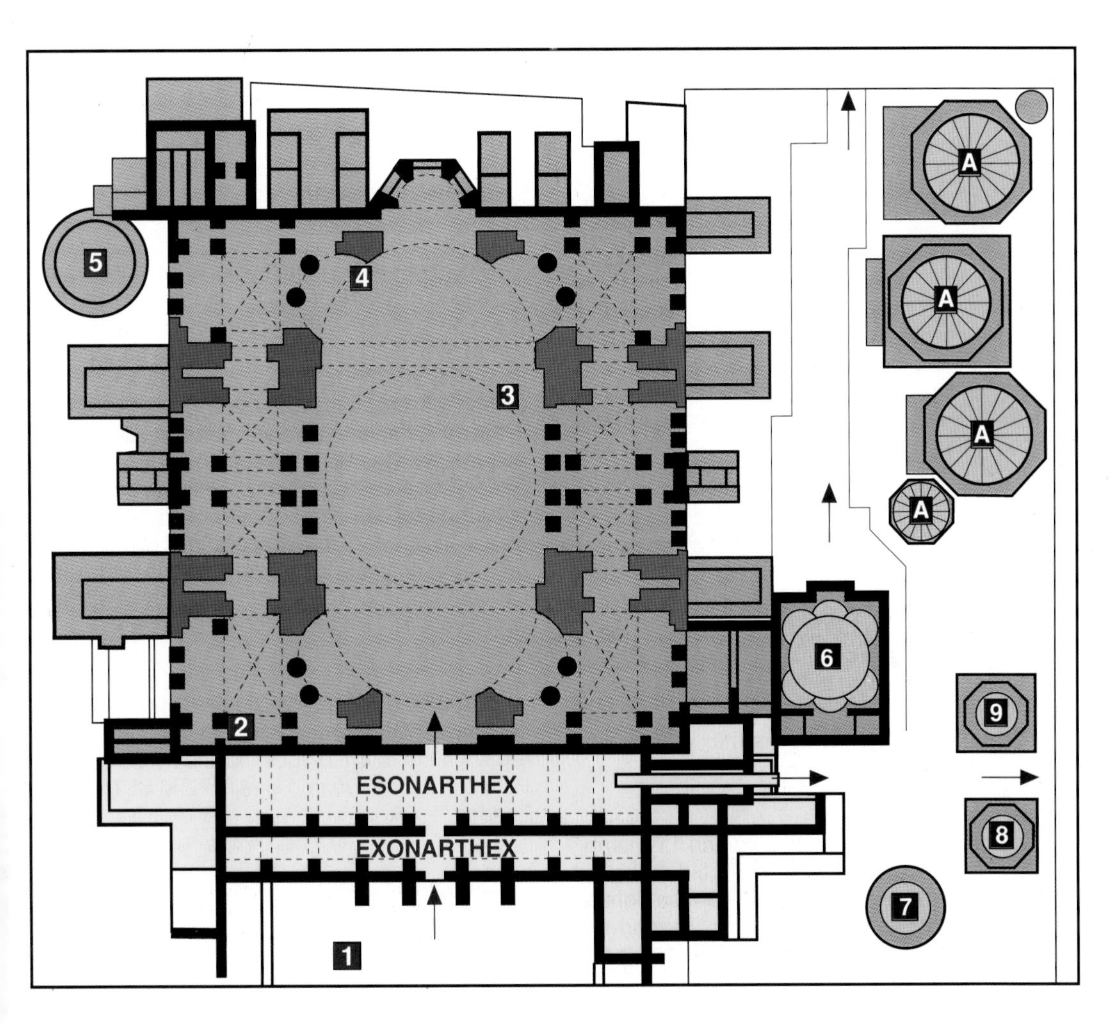

Ground plan of Haghia Sophia

1. *Theodosian Haghia Sophia (Excavations)*
2. *The moist column*
3. *The choirs' platform*
4. *Sultan's pulpit*
5. *Treasury*
6. *The old baptistery, now türbe of the sultans*
7. *The fountain*
8. *The elementary school*
9. *The clock house*

A. *Graves (türbe) of the sultans and princes*

ios of Tralles and Isidoros of Miletus were appointed to be the masters. The basilica with a grand dome was completed after five years and was formally dedicated by Justinian on December 26th 537. As he entered the church, filled with joy, he thanked God for letting him finish such a great masterpiece and said: "I have outdone you Solomon!" After twenty years in 557 the dome collapsed. Justinian I, who was still alive, appointed Isidoros' nephew to restore the church. When the job was finished, the dome was smaller and higher than before to lessen its outward thrust. On December 24th 563 Justinian, now an old man in the last months of his life, dedicated the church once again. In the following years the church was restored many times. In 1317 Emperor Andronikos Polaeologus fortified the walls. Right after the conquest the Turks added the minarets. In 1573 Sinan and his students built the first buttresses. Extensive restoration was carried out in the reign of Sultan Abdülmecit I by the Swiss architects, the brothers Fossati (1847-1849). In 1934 Atatürk had Haghia Sophia converted into a museum and made scientific research possible. Since then, the American Byzantine Institute has cleaned many mosaics. Haghia Sophia is a domed basilica and consists of a...

a) hall with exonarthex and narthex
b) central room with three naves and a gallery
c) garden surrounding the building.

Now we'll visit the church following the abovementioned order. From the western end we enter the exonarthex through the ancient entrance; five bronze gates connect the exonarthex with the narthex. The gates are decorated with cross motives.

The narthex is 60 metres long and 11 metres wide. The ceiling is covered with gold mosaics, and marble panels cover its walls. On the right of the narthex is the public entrance; beyond the gate you see a beautiful mosaic which depicts the enthroned Mother of God holding the Chirst-Child in her lap as she receives two emperors in audience. On her left "Constantine the Great Emperor among the Saints" offers her a model of the city of Constantinople; while "Justinian the Illustrious Emperor" on her right presents her with a model of Haghia Sophia.(10th c.) The exit gate dating from the second century was brought from a temple in Tarsus where Paulus was born.

In the lunette above the Imperial Gate, which leads from the narthex to the central room, we see a fabulous mosaic from the ninth century. It shows Christ seated upon a jewelled throne, his feet resting on a footstool. He raises His right hand in a gesture of blessing and in His left He holds a book in which we may read this inscription in Greek: "Peace be with you. I am the Light of the World". On Christ's right, Emperor Leo VI prostrates himself. Above, on either side of the throne, are two roundels depicting the Blessed Virgin and the archangel Gabriel.

Today we have none of the mosaics from Justinian's time because they were destroyed by the Iconoclasts (729-843).

Nine gates with strong hooks to hang thick curtains lead to the centre of the church.The first impression created by the interior of Haghia Sophia is that of a vast contained space. It's hard to believe that ten thousand workers built this grand church with the tools of their time in only five years. In the construction no wood scaffolding was used. As the Egyptians did in the construction of the pyramids, soil was heaped up. Justinian has to get the credit for the short construction period, because he divided the workers into two groups, promising bonuses to the faster one. In history the concept of piece-work must have started with the construction of Haghia Sophia.

In front of us, stands a domed basilica that occupies a 77 metre-long-and 71.20 metre-wide area. It's the fourth biggest basilica following St. Peters in Rome, Doumo in Milan and St. Pauls in London.

The immense dome, which is built of light bricks from Rhodes, is 55.60 metres high and 31-32 metres wide, and is supported by four enormous columns. With its 40 windows the dome gives you the impression that it is hanging in the air. The two semi-domes to east and west make it possible to appreciate the hovering height. Each of the pendentives of the main dome have the fresco of «Cherubim».

The space under the dome is the centre of the church. In the basement there are four granite co-

The interior of Haghia Sophia

lumns from Ephesus. The round niches in the corners have porphyry columns from the Apollo temple of Baalbec. Many of the columns have Byzantine capitals which have the surface decoration of acanthus and are generally known as bowl-type. At front and back the columns have the monograms of Justinian and Theodora. The marble panels on the walls were brought from the island of Marmara from which the word "marmor" is derived.

The mosaic floor in the south-east section of the main nave shouldn't be missed. Coronation ceremonies for the Byzantine emperors must have taken place here.

The north-west pillar in the north aisle is the famous moist column, and is believed to be miraculous.

The Mosaics in the nave

In the conch of the apse is the most beautiful mosaic depicting the Mother of God with the Christ Child on her knees (9th c.).

At the bottom of the arch we see another mosaic which shows a colossal figure -five metres high- of the archangel Gabriel who has one of his wings missing.

Opposite, on the north side of the arch, there should be a mosaic of Michael, but it has been In completely destroyed. (9th c.)

Three other mosaic portraits are located in niches at the base of the main arch: On the left St. Ignatius, in the middle St. John Chrysostom, on the right St. Ignatius Theophorus.

Mosaics in the gallery
A few mosaics remain in the gallery which was

Mosaic with Jesus, Constantine IX and Zoe

Part of the Deesis, Christ as the Pantocrator

the women's section. The oldest among them represents Alexander, son of Basileus I (10th c.) in the northern gallery.

In the south gallery there are two mosaics side by side. The left one depicts Empress Zoe with her third husband Constantine IX (Monomachos). In the centre we see Christ, his right hand raised in a gesture of benediction. The faces are interesting to examine closely. Zoe, who was already 50 years old at the time of her first marriage, is shown like a twenty year old. With every marriage of the empress the head and the name of the former husband had to be replaced. Those changes are clearly visible on the mosaic.

To the right of the above-mentioned mosaic we see the Mother of God holding the infant Christ; to her right stands Emperor John Comnenus and to her left stands Empress Eirene (12th c.) and their son Alexius.

The most magnificent mosaic in the gallery is

Mosaic of the Mother of God with John II Comnenus and Eirene

the Deesis, which is located in the loge of the empress (14th c.).It shows Christ flanked by the Virgin and St. John the Baptist. Opposite to the Deesis is the tomb of the Venetian Doge Henricus Dandalo who was the leader of the Fourth Crusade.

Islamic-Turkish decorations

The mihrab (prayer niche) was placed in the direction of Mecca. The gigantic candlesticks standing on its sides were donated by Sultan Süleyman I and were made in Hungary. The imperial log to the left of the apse was constructed by Gaspar Fossati (19th c.). The marble preacher's throne is located in the middle of the northern arcade. In the 16th century Sultan Murat brought the marble basins from the island of Marmara. The congregation uses them to perform their ablutions. The eight huge green panels hanging in the central room contain the Holy Names of Allah, the Prophet Mohammed, the four Caliphs and Mohammed's grandchildren.

The garden of Haghia Sophia

To the south there is a domed structure from the 19th century which was the workshop of the mosque astronomer. The treasure of the church used to be stored in the building in the north-east. The other domed buildings are the "türbes" of the sultans and princes.

To the west are ruins of marble columns and a Theodosian church. In front of the Imperial Gate is the entrance to the Theodosian church, which was uncovered during the excavations in 1935. To the south-west corner of the yard is a beautiful fountain, a pretty example of Turkish rococo style of the 18th century. At the southern entrance (today's exit), lies the Justinian Baptistry which now shelters the graves of the sultans.

The Hippodrome

The Hippodrome (At Meydanı) D5

The Roman Emperor Septimius Severus built this place which lies to the west of the Blue Mosque, in the year 203. Emperor Constantine the Great extended it later.

During the Byzantine era the Hippodrome was the centre of civil activities. Not only chariot races and gladiator fights, but also celebrations in honour of the emperor took place here. Twice it was the site of bloody battles and riots. The first riot started between the two political parties (the Greens and the Blues) during Justinian's reign in the year 532. It almost cost Justinian his throne; but his general Belisarius slaughtered 40.000 rebels in the Hippodrome. The second slaughter took place when Sultan Mahmut II ordered the execution of 30.000 rebellious janissaries at the same place.

The Hippodrome is approximately 400m in length and 120m in width and seated 40.000 spectators according to one estimate. The entrance was located about where the fountain of emperor Wilhelm II is now. Along the sides, step-like seats were placed, and the Hippodrome had a semi-circular southern end called the sphendone. An arcade of columns marked the upper end of this semi-circle, where four bronze-gilt horses once stood (now they are in Museo Marciano); as Constantine the Great had them brought from Rome. In 1204, Doge Enrico Dandolo towed them as war-booty to Venice, where they stood on top of the main gate of the church Marcus.

The central line of the race-course, a strong and long wall, the so-called "spina" was decorated with obelisks and columns, few of which are still standing.

The imperial lodge "kathisma" was located in the middle of the eastern side of the arena, and could only be entered from the palace. The lower floor of the enclosure was for the band and the guards.

The Hippodrome

The Serpent Colun

1- The Egyptian Obelisk (Dikilitaş)

This obelisk was erected by the Egyptian king Thutmose III at Deir el Bahri in the (15th c. B.C.) About two thousand years later Emperor Theodosius I. brought the monolith to Istanbul in the year of 390, and it was erected on the spina with a ceremony. The 20 metre-high obelisk is mounted on four brazen blocks, which rest on a marble base with sculpted reliefs.

The east side: Emperor Theodosius is sitting in his box with a head wreath in his hand, with which he is to honour the winner of the horse race. At his sides stand his sons Arcadius and Honorius. Behind him is his body guard, and the spectators, the dancers and the musicians are depicted beneath.

The north side: (Opposite the fountain of Emperor Wilhelm II)

On the lower block the erection of the obelisk is represented whereas on the upper part we see the emperor and his household.

The west side: The emperor is receiving homage from vanquished enemies. Below, there are two envoys presenting their gifts.

The south side: In the upper part Emperor Theodosius is shown with his family, body guards, and spectators in his box during the competition. The lower one shows the race course of the Hippodrome. Inscriptions in Greek and Latin on the base, praise Theodosius and his prefect Proclus.

II- The Serpent Column(Burmalı Sütun)

This column is the oldest Greek monument in Istanbul. In 479 B.C. it was erected by 31 cities, which defeated the Persians in the battle of Plataea, in memorandum of the victory in the Temple of Apollo at Delphi. The names of the cities are inscribed on the coils of the serpents near the bottom. According to tradition, the bronze serpents were cast from the shields of the fallen Persian warriors.

The column is five metres high and represents three thick intertwined serpents. The missing upper part of the column consisted of a tripod carrying a golden bowl.

The upper part of one of the serpent heads is now on exhibit on the second floor of the Archaelogical Museum.

The Egyptian Obelisk-north side

The Egyptian Obelisk-west side

III- The Colossus (Örmeli Sütun)

Emperor Constantine VII Porphyrogenitus erected this column made of lime stone in the year 940. The earlier bronze-gilt facing which depicted farmers and fishermen, was torn off by the Fourth Crusaders and melted. Today you can still notice the holes of the panels in the stone.

Chora Church (Kariye Müzesi) B4

We know that there was a Justinian monastery at this site. It was called "Chora" (in the country) because the ancient monastery to which it was attached was outside the Constantinian walls. In the year 558, an earthquake which also caused the dome of Haghia Sophia to collapse, destroyed it completely, but it was reconstructed immediately and existed till the Iconoclasts damaged it.

The present building dates from the late eleventh century and was built by Maria Doukaina, mother-in law of the Emperor Alexius I Comnenus, between the years 1077 and 1081. His grandson Isaac Comnenus remodelled the damaged church in the year 1120. It didn't last long in this form because the crusaders tore it down. Detailed restoration became essential, and this was carried out by Theodor Metochites, the Grand Logothete (the highest official of the emperor). In 1313 he enlarged the church, adding the exonarthex and the parecclesion. He also decorated the nave with mosaics and frescos. According to tradition, after his service he became a monk in the same church where he was later buried following his death.

After the conquest of the city by the Turks, the church was converted into a mosque in 1500. The mosaics and frescos were cleaned and preserved by the Byzantine Institute of America between the years 1948 and 1959. Since then it's been a museum.

Its mosaics and frescoes depict scenes from the lives of the Mother of God ant Christ. They date from the early 14th century. From an artistic point of view, Kariye is a beautiful example of the beginning of the Byzantine Renaissance. Although the building is small and inconspicuous, the interior deserves special attention for the mosaics and frescoes.

The mosaics in the exonarthex

1- The twelve year old Christ in the Temple (Christ with scribes)

2- Joseph's dream, the journey to Bethlehem

Chora-Church (Kariye Müzesi)

Ground plan of Chora Church (Kariye Müzesi)

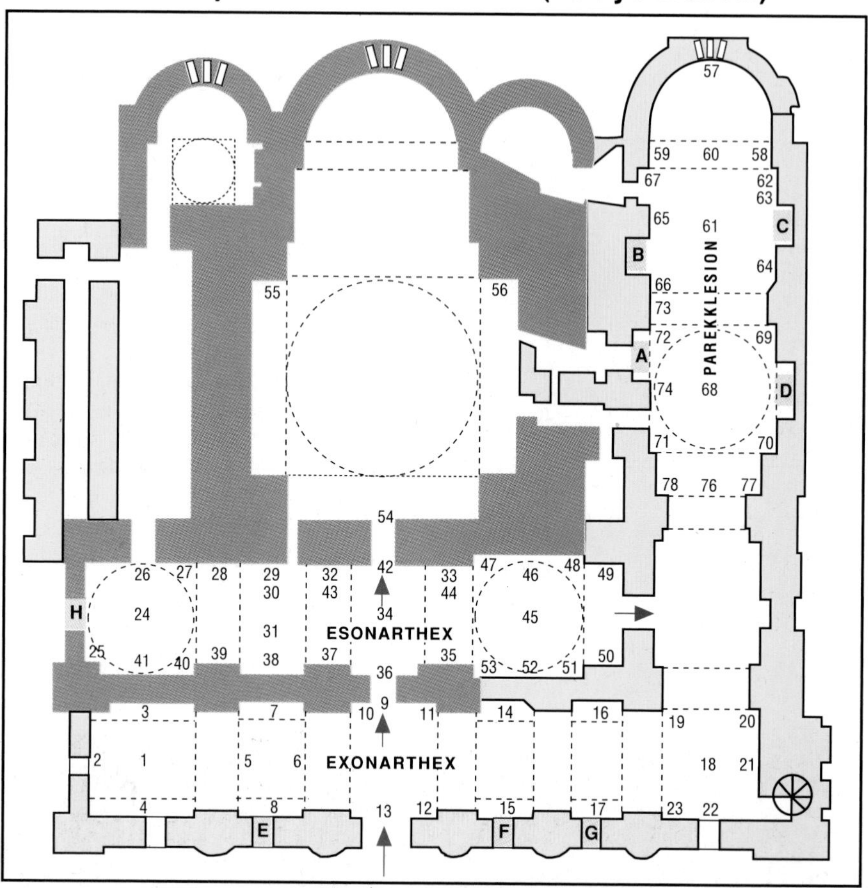

3- Joseph and the Virgin at the census before Cyrenius, the Syrian governor.

4- The twelve year old Christ on the journey to Jerusalem.

5- John the Baptist bearing witness for Christ.

6- The Temptation of Christ.

7- The Birth of Christ.

8- Joseph's dream and the return of the Holy Family to Nazareth.

9- Christ Pantocrator (the Almighty).

10- The Miracle at Cana.

11-12 The multiplication of the Loaves.

13- The Virgin and the Angel.

14- The three wise men from the East on their way to Jerusalem ask Herod about the birth place of Christ.

15- The flight of Elizabeth with John the Baptist (The mountains open to receive her and protect her from Herod).

16- Herod enquiring of the Priests and Scribes after Christ's birthplace.

17- Mothers mourning their children.

18-19- Christ healing the Paralytic at the Pool of Bethesda.

20- Christ healding the Hydrophilic.

21-22- The Massacre of the children at Bethlehem (Herod deceived by the wise men demands children of the age of two and under to be killed).

23- Christ and the Samaritan Woman.

Mosaics in the inner narthex:

24- The Virgin in the middle, Christ's ancestors in the flutes.

Chora Church

25- Joachim's Offerings Rejected (badly damaged, only the Virgin before Zacharias, the High Priest, can be seen)

26- The Annunciation to St. Anne (the angel of the Lord announcing to Anne that her prayer for a child has been heard)

27- Joachim in the Wilderness (Ashamed at the rejection of his offerings, Joachim goes into the wilderness to pray for offspring.)

28- The meeting of Joachim and Anne in Jerusalem

29- The Birth of the Blessed Virgin

30- The Virgin caressed by her Parents (the two magnificent peacocks represent incorruptibility

31- Joachim presents the Virgin to the High Priests at the Temple

32- The first steps of the Virgin when she was six months old

33- The Virgin receiving Bread from Gabriel

34- At the age of three the Virgin was presented at the Temple where she stayed nine years.

35- The Virgin is instructed at the Temple

36- The Virgin receiving the skein of purple wool for the Temple veil

37- Zacharias praying before the Rods of the Suitors (they are the widowers asking for the Virgin's hand in marriage)

38- Joseph with the sprouting rod (the Virgin is entrusted to Joseph)

39- Joseph taking the Virgin to his House

40- The Annunciation to the Virgin at the Well

41- Joseph taking leave of the Virgin

42- Theodore Metochites presenting his church to Christ

43- St. Peter

The dome of the inner narthex with golden mosaics

44- St. Paul

45- In the crown a medallion of Christ Pantocrator, and in the flutes his ancestors

46- The Deesis with Isaac Comnenus and Melane (probably it represents Maria, half-sister of Andronicus Palaeologus, who is known to be the queen of the Mongols. Melane (black) was her religious name.)

47- Christ healing Peter's Mother-in-Law

48- Christ healing the Women with the Issue of Blood

49- Christ healing the Man with the Withered Hand

50- Christ healing the Leper

51- Christ healing the Deaf and Dumb Man

52- Christ healing various diseases

53- Christ healing the two Blind Men of Jericho

Mosaics in the nave

54- The Dormition (Koimesis) of the Virgin. The Virgin lies dead on her bier. Behind her stands Christ holding her soul. Over Christ's head hovers a six-winged seraph. Around stand the apostles and bishops.

55- Christ with the gospel

56- The Virgin with the Christ child

Frescoes in the parecclesion:

57- The Anastasis (Resurrection) (Christ pulls Adam and Eve out of their tombs. Beneath his feet the bound Satan lies in front of the broken-down gates of Hell, and behind are the prophets.

58- Christ raising the Daughter of Jairus

59- Christ raising the Widow's Son of Naim

60- The Archangel Michael

61- The Last Judgement (Christ in the centre as the Universal Judge. Below are depicted the souls of the saved. The condemned souls are going to Hell. Below to left a River of Fire broadens to a lake where Lucifer is waiting for the damned.)

The Dormition of the Virgin

62- The Rich Man in Hell appeals to Lazarus for water

63- The Torments of the Damned

64- The Land and Sea giving up the Dead

65- The Entry of the Elect into Paradise (St. Peter leads the saved souls into Paradise where John the Baptist is shown with the angels.)

66- An Angel conducts the Soul of Lazarus to Heaven

67- Lazarus the Beggar in Abraham's Bosom

68- The Virgin with the Christ child and 12 angels around her

69- St. Cosmas the Poet
70- St.Joseph the Poet
71- St. Theophanes the Confessor
72- St. John Damascene
] Hymnographers

73- Moses and the Burning Bush (The angel of the Lord says: "Moses, you're on holy ground, take off your shoes." On the adjacent mosaic Moses is hiding his face; he's afraid to look upon God.)

74- Jacob's Ladder and Jacob wrestling with the Angel

75-a- The priests took up the Ark of the Covenant to bring it out of the city of David, "Sion."

75b- The King and all Israel were assembled before the Ark.

75c- The Ark of the Lord is brought into the Temple of Solomon

76- The Souls of the Righteous in the Hand of God (badly damaged)

77- Isaiah and the Angel (The King of Assyria is not allowed to enter Jerusalem)

78- Aaron and his Sons bring their offerings before the Altar

The tombs in the parecclesion:

A- Probably it's the tomb of Theodor Metochites (it lost its identifying inscription)

B and C- The inscriptions are lost.

D- The tomb of Michael Tornikes, general and friend of Metochites.

The tombs in the outer narthex:

E and F- cannot be identified

G- tomb of the Princess Irene Palaeologina

The tomb in the inner narthex:

H- tomb of Demetrius Doukas Angleus Palaeologus

Wedding at Cana

Christ healing St. Peter's mother-in-law

The parecclesion (side chapel)

The Church of Pammakaristos

The Church of Pammakaristos (Fethiye Camii Müzesi) B4

The main church, which now serves as a mosque, was erected by Emperor John Comnenus in the 12th century. In the 13th century it was reconstructed by Michael Glabas, the protostrator (the highest official in the Byzantine empire). After he passed away, his wife Maria Dukas donated a side chapel, the parecclesion with four columns and a gallery,at the-south east of the church at the beginning of the 14th century. In the 14th century the church became a nunnery. Following the conquest of Istanbul by the Turks, the Orthodox Patriarchate lived there for 130 years, after the Patriarch Gennadius abandoned the Church of the Holy Apostles. In the year 1591 Sultan Murat III converted the church into a mosque and named it "Fethiye Camii" (mosque of the victory) to commemerate his conquest of Georgia and Azerbaijan. Since then it has served as a mosque, only the side chapel at the south is used as a museum.

The building consists of a central church with a narthex. In about the year 1300, an outer narthex and a side chapel (parecclesion) on the south were added, and it served as a burial site to the Comnenus family for years.

Parecclesion (side chapel)

This miniature domed church consists of a triple arcade with three apses and a narthex. On the upper floor is the women's section with two small towers. Today the church is considered to be one of the most attractive buildings of the Byzantine period.

In the meantime, the chapel has been beautifully restored, and in the interior, fragments of

Christ and four archangels

stained glass and mosaics have survived. The mosaics date back to the 14th century and depict the following scenes:

The dome mosaic shows Christ Pantocrator surrounded by twelve prophets. In the apse we see Christ "Hyperagathos" with the Virgin, John the Baptist and archangels (Michael, Gabriel, Raphael, Uriel). To the east of the central dome, the baptism of Christ is depicted. In the corners and arches, a few saints and the Early Fathers are to be seen.

On the facade of the side chapel two inscriptions can be read. The first inscription placed with bricks is in the middle of the southern side of the chapel.

The second inscription is placed on the ledge which separates the storeys from each other and belongs to the popular poet Manuel Philes. (14th c. A.D.)

Christ with twelve prophets

Haghia Eirene (Aya Irini Kilisesi) D5

Haghia Eirene (Church of the Divine Peace) is one of the oldest Christian sanctuaries in the city. In the 4th century Constantine the Great built the church on the site of a Temple to Aphrodite and dedicated it to the Holy Peace. Until Haghia Sophia was built, Haghia Eirene served as the partriarchal cathedral of the city. Here the second Oecumenical Council held its meeting, during the reign of Emperor Theodosius I in the year 381. During the Nika Revolt in 532 Haghia Eirene was destroyed by fire, but after five years it was re-dedicated. Following the earthquake in 740 Constantine V had it restored. After the Conquest Haghia Eirene was enclosed within the outer walls of Topkapı Palace and served as an arsenal. In the nineteenth century the first collection of antiques was stored in the church, and till 1950 it was used as a military exhibit. Haghia Eirene has the status of a museum, and exhibitions or concerts will be crganized here from time to time.

The church is a basilica. The apse, semi-circular within, five-sided without, has a semi-dome above. In the semi-dome of the apse there are fragments of a mosaic of a cross against a gold background. On the walls in the central dome and even in the narthex we see mosaic fragments. In the front yard, which is adjacent to the narthex, a porphyry sarcophagus associated with Constantine the Great draws our attention.

Haghia Eirene

The central dome of Süleymaniye Mosque

MOSQUES (Selection)

Süleymaniye Mosque (Süleymaniye Camii) C5

This mighty mosque was built during the reign of Sultan Süleyman 1 (the Magnificent) after his return from the victory in Hungary, by the architect «Sinan» in the years 1550-1557. Without doubt, it's the most important Ottoman building in Istanbul. One has to consider the fact that Süleyman the Magnificent decided to construct a mosque after thirty years on the throne; that's why he intended it to be unique.

The mosque stands on one of the seven hills of Istanbul. It was built inside the perimeter of the oldest sultan's palace, which doesn't exist today. The mosque consists of an outer courtyard, an inner courtyard and a prayer room with a dome. Apart from these three areas, the outer courtyard is surrounded by buildings, which once served as the academy, caravansaray, the hospital, the poor-kitchen and the baths.

We first enter the outer courtyard. To the right we see the washing facilities, where Moslems perform the cleansing ritual prior to praying five times a day. Farther down to the left we enter the inner courtyard, where 24 antique columns of porphyry, marble and granite, support 28 domes, and a rectangular marble fountain (Şadırvan) stands in the centre. All these columns originate from the Hippodrome. On certain religious holidays or for Friday prayers (the main prayer that corresponds to the Christian Sunday service) when there is no place to pray in the crowded mosque, people pray in this courtyard on straw mats.

Above the main gate that leads into the mosque, there is an Arabic inscription: «There is no God but Allah, and Mohammed is his prophet.» Four minarets in the corners of the inner courtyard show that Süleyman the Manificent was the fourth sultan since the conquest of Istanbul, whereas the ten balconies that he was the tenth ruler of the Ottoman Empire.

Upon entering the mosque its beauty and harmony capture your attention. The ground plan of the mosque is a rectangle of 57m ×60m. The central dome that covers the entire interior is 53m. high and has a diameter of 27.50m. Four strong piers support this huge dome, and to the east and west the dome is supported by semi-domes 40m. high and with diameters of 23m. The dome-arches rise from four great piers. Between the piers triple arcades on two monolithic columns support the tympana of the arches. One of those columns was the Column of Virginity erected in the surroundings of the Apostle Church in Istanbul. The second one originates from the imperial palaces near Haghia Sophia, and the other two are from Alexandrette (Iskenderun).

The decorative inscriptions are by the famous calligrapher Ahmet Karahisari and his student Hasan Çelebi. On the east wall there are wonderful stained-glass windows. They were attached with goat hair and egg white, and gypsum was used for the frames. They are masterpieces made by the artist known as «İbrahim the Drunkard».

The Fossati brothers illuminated the central dome in the last century in the style of the Ottoman baroque patterns. The mihrab (prayer niche), sultan's lodge and mimber (Friday pulpit) in Proconnesian marble, are of great simplicity. The woodwork of the preacher's chair inlaid with ivory and mother-of-pearl, and the window shutters are noteworthy.

The galleries on the sides weren't reserved for women as in the sultan's mosque, but for the noble. The acoustics in the mosque are marvellous. It's said that the architect Sinan put pipes in the ground from the mihrab to every corner of the mosque, to enable the prayer and the preaching of the imam (person who leads in prayer) to be

Süleymaniye Mosque

heard outside the mosque as well.

The black globes hanging under the central dome are black ostrich eggs, which have no religious meaning. Their odour must be a repellent against spiders. To prevent spider webs in this spacious room, they were changed every year before they dried out.

Since there was no electricity in the sixteenth century, the mosque was illuminated with hundreds of oil lamps. The burning of the oil caused large soot particles which formed balls under the dome. Above the door in a niche Sinan made little windows, through which the ball of soot was drawn into another room. Humidity was very dense because of the breath of approximately 5000 believers in the mosque, and it was precipitated onto the wall. In those days the best ink was made out of this precipitation.

To the east of the mosque there is an interesting cemetery, where the türbes (graves) of Süleyman I and his Russian wife Roxelane are located.

Evliya Çelebi, the most famous Turkish traveller of the sixteenth century, who collected his memoirs in book form, tells us that the high minaret with three balconies to the left of the main entrance was called «Jewel Minaret» and the reason is explained as follows: The construction of the mosque was delayed when Süleyman wanted to devote himself to his civic duties. The Persian shah «Tahmasp» heard the news, and sent a messenger with a box full of priceless jewels to the sultan. In his letter he wrote: "I've heard that you cannot continue the construction of your mosque because of financial problems. Convert these stones into cash and finish the building soon. This is how I can take part in your pious work." The letter made the sultan furious. He gave the box to Sinan and said: "These precious stones have no value beside the stones of my mosque. Mix the stones with the others to built the minaret." Sınan used the jewels in the construction of the minaret and that's why it's called the "Jewel Minaret".

Minarets of the Süleymaniye Mosque

The central dome seen from the interior

Sinan's Life (1490-1588)

According to various sources, Sinan (the most famous Turkish architect) was from the province of Kayseri, ancient Caesarea, and he was taken away from his family at the age of 21 to be one of the inductees at the sultan's disposal. At the age of 25 he joined the Guards, and was assigned to the Janissaries. Later he came to the palace of İbrahim Pasha (at the Hippodrome) for apprenticeship and stayed there for a few years.

In the army Sinan was the pioneer officer who learned the art of carpentry, and he was also a master of stone-masonry and war construction. In 1539 at the age of 49, after being appointed Chief of the Imperial Architects by Sultan Süleyman I, who appreciated his great talent, Sinan created his magnificent buildings. In his lifetime he built 80 big mosques and 50 small mosques, many schools, hospitals, palaces, bridges, aqueducts and Turkish baths. In all they are 320 structures.

He died in the year 1588 and was buried to the northeast of the mosque outside the outer courtyard in a simple grave.

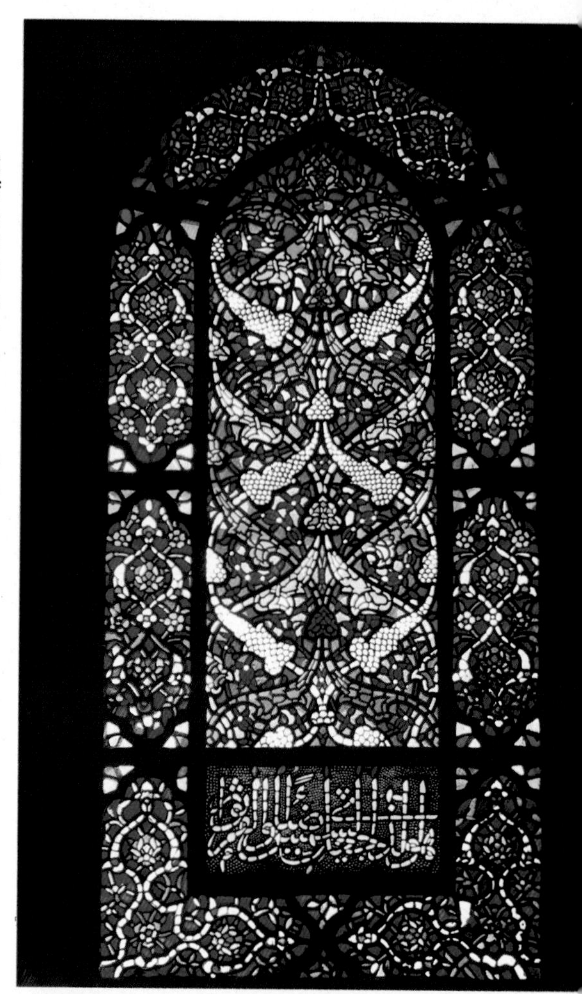

A colourful stained glasswindow on the south-east wall

Interior of the Süleymaniye Mosque

Blue Mosque

The Blue Mosque or the Sultan Ahmet Mosque D5

One of the most beautiful and grand mosques in Istanbul rises to the east of «At Meydanı», the old Hippodrome, opposite Haghia Sophia. It was founded by Sultan Ahmet I, who was twenty years old then, as a counterpoint to Haghia Sophia and was constructed by the architect Mehmet Aga, one of Sinan's students. Because of its blue-green tiles it is also called the Blue Mosque.

The sultans used the mosque as the scene of important religious declarations. Here religious holidays were celebrated, and from here the pilgrims started their journey to Mecca.

The Blue Mosque is the only mosque with six minarets in the world. The legend is as follows: Before Sultan Ahmet I left for Mecca, he told his architect to build golden minarets for the mosque. From the financial point of view, the master found the order impossible and used the unison of the words "gold" and "six" ("Altın" and "Altı") and built six stone minarets.

Like the Süleymaniye Mosque the Blue Mosque also has three parts: The outer courtyard, the inner courtyard and the domed central building.

To the west you enter through a gate in the outer yard. On the gate a metal chain is hanging; in token of his respect for God, the sultan had to bow every time he rode his horse through the gate.

Through a beautiful gate decorated with stalactite motives we reach the inner courtyard, which has the same dimensions as the prayer hall, 64m

The Blue Mosque viewed from the north

× 72m. The courtyard is bordered by 26 granite columns, with stalactite capitals forming a portico covered by 30 small domes. At the centre of the courtyard there is an octagonal fountain. Three gates lead into the mosque; the one leading to the inner courtyard is the grandest. The interior which is nearly a square presents a centralized architect's plan. 260 windows, which were once filled with coloured glass, light up the interior of the mosque throughout the day. During Ramadan, when the lights brighten the blue-green tiles and the red carpets, the mosque interior looks fascinating.

The central dome is 43m. high and has a diameter of 23.5m. Four round piers covered with marble plates support the dome, and on each side it's supported by semi-domes.

A gallery (women's mezzanine) supported by columns has the best tiles in the mosque on its walls, and borders the prayer hall on three sides. On the lower part of the walls and in the galleries, the interior is revetted with 21.000 tiles from Iznik (ancient Nikaia) from the 17th century. The magnificent floral designs display the traditional lily, carnation, tulip and rose motives and also cypresses in blue, green and brown tones. Since Islam forbids the representation of God in a human form, there are no human motives. The upper part of the walls and vaults are painted with colourful ornaments, and the dominant colour is blue. The marvellous calligraphs, and the arabesques in bronze-gilt colour are also noteworthy. The mihrab (prayer niche) and mimber (Friday pulpit) of white Proconnesian marble are original; and are fine examples of the carved stonework of the period. The woodwork, encrusted with ivory and mother-of-pearl, of the doors, window-shutters and the sermon chair are also excellent. The marble sultan's lodge with the bronze-gilt bars is beautiful and valuable.

In the outer courtyard of the mosque there are buildings such as the türbe (grave) of Sultan Ahmet I, the former medrese (koran school) in the north-west, and in the south-east, a small sultan's pavilion with direct access to the sultan's lodge. Since 1978 an interesting museum of rugs has been placed in the pavilion.

The Interior of the Blue Mosque

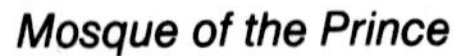

Mosque of the Prince

Mosque of the Conqueror

Mosque of the Prince (Şehzade Camii) C5

In 1544-1548, Süleyman the Magnificent had the architect Sinan build this mosque as an expiatory monument, in the honour of the crown prince Mehmet, who was killed upon his order.

The Mosque of the Prince was the first grand mosque built in 1539 in Istanbul by Sinan, who was appointed Chief of the Architects. He called it his "apprentice work".

The mosque has a square ground-plan and resembles Byzantine churches in many respects. Four strong octangular piers called "elephant's feet" support the dome, which is 37m high and has a diameter of 18m. As for the interior decoration, the colourful windows and the richly ornamented pulpit are noteworthy.

In the square front courtyard, 12 marble and granite columns support 16 domes, which cover the arcade around the yard. Two geometrical minarets flank the building, surrounded by an old Koran school and a caravanserai . Today there is a rooming house for students at this site. The türbes (graves) of Prince Mehmet and Grand Vizier Rüstem Pasha are located in the outer courtyard.

Mosque of the Conqueror (Fatih Camii) B4

After the conquest of Istanbul, this mosque was built by the architect Atik Sinan in the reign of Sultan Mehmet II (the Conqueror), at the site of the Church of the Holy Apostles, in the years 1463-1470. The mosque was destroyed in an earthquake and was reconstructed in baroque style by the architect Mehmet Tahir in the years 1767-1771.

In the front courtyard, 18 antique columns support 22 domes. A beautiful fountain with a conical roof decorates the centre of the courtyard, which is surrounded by trees.

There are three mezzanines in the mosque, and the central dome is flanked by four semidomes on the axes. Again we see the plan that Sinan used in the construction of the Mosque of the Prince, the Blue Mosque and the Mosque of the Sultan's Mother. In the garden adjacent to the mosque, are the türbes of Mehmet II, his wife "Gülbahar" and Abdülhamit I.

The entire area occupied by the mosque with the attendant buildings (library, primary school, eight Koran schools, hospital, hospice and Turkish bath) extends over 100sq.m and represents the largest mosque complex in Istanbul.

Beyazit Mosque

Portrait of Mehmet II (the Conqueror) 15th century

Beyazit Mosque (Beyazit Camii) C5

The architect Hayrettin built this mosque during the reign of Beyazit II, son and successor of Mehmet II the Conqueror, during 1497-1505. This mosque is the oldest among the Sultans' mosques. Because of the doves that live at the mosque it is also known as the Dove Mosque. It's said that the doves come from a pair sold by an old man to the Sultan.

In the square front courtyard 20 antique columns support 24 domes. The ablution fountain in the centre dates back to the 17th century.

A grand dome supported by two semi-domes over the niche and the doorway, roofs the central hall. The other rooms are each covered by four small domes. The mosque represents a transition from the early Ottoman style with piers to the classical form. From an architectural point of view, it is a very interesting mosque.

In the cemetery in the south-eastern garden are the türbe of Beyazıt II and two other tombs. The additional buildings of the mosque are now housing the public library.

The interior of the Mosque of Rüstem Paşa

Rüstem Paşa Mosque
(Rüstem Paşa Camii) C5

Grand Vizier Rüstem Pasha, husband of Süleyman's (the Magnificent) favourite daughter, built this pretty mosque in the business district of Eminönü on the Golden Horn in 1561. As far as the quality of its architecture and the tile decoration are concerned, among Sinan's smaller works it's one of the most beautiful mosques in Istanbul.

The mosque consists of a domed hall, with three side halls and a front courtyard. The walls of the interior, and the octangular piers are sheathed with Iznik tiles. Besides that, the walls of the lobby are covered with the fine blue-green Iznik tiles which represent the most beautiful examples of tile art in the 16th century.

Mosque of Princess Mihrimah

Mihrimah Mosque
(Mihrimah Camii) B4

This mosque was built by the famous architect Sinan for Mihrimah, the daughter of Süleyman the Magnificent and the wife of Grand Vizier Rüstem Pasha at the site of a church in 1555. In 1894 it was severely damaged in an earthquake; but in 1910 and 1958 it was restored.

The building (built on a platform) consists of a square domed hall with neighbouring halls that have three domes each. The 37m-high dome is 20 m in diameter, and is supported by four granite piers. Blue and red-brown colours on a white background dominate the interior. Daylight illuminates the mosque through the lunettes. Noteworthy, are the lunettes in the south-east, and so is the fine carved stonework of the mihrab and the mimber.

The front courtyard dates from the 18th century. Behind the domed arcade are the Koran schools. Near the courtyard is the mosque's lobby covered by 7 domes.

The attendant building of the mosque is a double Turkish bath.

The New Mosque of the Sultan's Mother

Nuruosmaniye Mosque

The New Mosque of the Sultan's Mother (Yeni Valide Camii) C4

The mosque was commissioned in 1597 by Valide Sultan Safiye, the mother of Sultan Mehmet III. Architect Davut Ağa started the construction at Galata Bridge, and it was completed in 1663 under the supervision of Valide Sultan Turhan Hatice, the mother of Mehmet IV.

Wide steps lead to the front courtyard on a paltform. The ablution fountain of the courtyard is considered to be the most beautiful one in Istanbul. A portico with 24 domes surrounds this yard.

The ground-plan resembles that of the Blue Mosque's. The building is centralized.The central dome is supported by four piers and is flanked by four semi-domes. The interior is decorated with tiles on the walls and the piers. A small separate royal pavilion is attached to the sultan's lodge, which is adorned with colourful lunettes, carved doors and fine tiles.

To the south are the türbes of the foundress and other sultans.

Nuruosmaniye Mosque (Nuruosmaniye Camii) C5

This baroque mosque stands in the busy business district at the entrance of the Grand Bazaar. It was begun by Sultan Mahmut I in 1748 and was completed by Sultan Osman in 1756. The architect was Simon Kalfa.

Flights of steps lead to the horseshoe-shaped courtyard, where 12 columns support 14 domes. Different from the other mosques in the city, this mosque doesn't have an ablution fountain.

A grand dome covers the square interior, which is illuminated by five rows of lunettes. Both minarets have stony profiled spires.

A medrese (Koran school), a public kitchen and a library with valuable inscriptions belong to the mosque complex.

The ablution fountain of Selim Mosque

Mosque of Selim

Selim Mosque (Yavuz Selim Camii) B4

Sultan Süleyman the Magnificent built this mosque in honour of his father Selim I, on one of the seven hills of the city during 1520-1522. The square building (25mx25m) is covered by a shallow dome. To the sides are the flanks covered by 9 domes each. The interior of the mosque is decorated with fine İznik tiles, and the carved stonework of mihrab and mimber is beautiful.. .. In the front courtyard, 18 columns support 22 domes. A marble fountain with curved roof embellishes the centre of the courtyard.

In the garden of the mosque are the türbes of Sultan Selim I, Sultan Abdülmecit (died in 1861) and four children of Süleyman II. The terrace offers a beautiful view of the Golden Horn.

The interior of the Sergius and Bacchus Church

The Sergius and Bacchus Church (Küçük Ayasofya Camii) C5

Before Justinian came to the throne he took part in a conspiracy against Emperor Anastasius and was sentenced to death. Before the execution, the saints Sergius and Bacchus appeared to the Emperor and asked him to reprieve conspirators. Later when Justinian became Emperor, he built this church to express his gratitude to the saints (527-536).

Sergius and Bacchus were two Roman legionar ies, who died as martyrs and became the patron saints of the Christians in the Roman army.

The church was near the palaces by the sea and belonged together with the neighbouring Peter and Paul Church to the cloister of Hormisdas.

At the beginning of the 16th century it was converted into a mosque. As a result, Islamic cultural influence became dominant.

The ground plan of this church is very unique; an octagon built in an irregular square. The piers of the octagon support the dome. Red and green antique columns, which have "melon" type capitals on the ground floor and "pseudo-Ionic" capitals in the gallery, and the marble decoration of the halls, show us the former splendour of this holy house. Between the basement and the gallery, an inscription praising Justinian and Theodora surrounds the prayer hall.

Justinian's architectural art, which is considered displayed in the first stage of Haghia Sophia, started with the Sergius and Bacchus Church.

The succeeding buildings are St. Vitale in Ravenna and the Chapel of Karl the Great in Aachen.

Aqueduct of Valens

AQUEDUCTS AND CISTERNS

The.aqueducts were built to feed the cisterns with water from springs, which were located right next to the city. The provision of water played an important role in a city like Istanbul, which was besieged frequently.. That's why, during the Byzantine and Turkish periods a lot of aqueducts were built. They took the water from the Belgrade Forest. (see page 112)

Valens Aqueduct (Bozdoğan Kemeri) 4C

It's the only aqueduct in the middle of the city, and was built during the reign of the Roman Emperor Valens in the 4th century. It connected the third and fourth hills of the city, and its end was a big well near the university; from where the water was distributed to the imperial palaces. The ancient two-storey aqueduct is 26m high, and used to be 1000m long; but today only 800m remain.

In the surroundings of Istanbul we have a lot of aqueducts of Byzantine and Turkish origin. They are located in the Belgrade Forest (see page 112) and near the Fresh. Waters of Europe. which flow into the Golden Horn.

Cisterns

The numerous cisterns in Istanbul illustrate the vital importance of these facilities. They provided the city with water during times of peace and times of war. There are two kinds of cisterns: open cisterns and covered cisterns.

Open cisterns are usually located on hills and were built as ponds. Probably they were the purification plants of the covered cisterns, and provided the city with water.

Noterworthy are the following: **Cistern of Aetios** of the 5th century. Today it's a sports stadium «Vefa Stadyumu». (plan B4)

Cistern of Bonus is located to the north of the Selim Mosque and now serves as a garden (5th century) (plan B4). **Cistern of Mocius** is located in the neighbourhood "Altımermer" and is only a ditch today (6th century) (plan B5).

Covered Cisterns are few in Istanbul. Either the rain or the springs fed them. Most of these cisterns are domed underground halls with columns. Because of their artistic splendour I'd like to describe two covered cisterns as beautiful examples built during Justinian's reign:

The underground cistern "Yerebatan Sarayı"

The Underground Palace (Yerebatan Sarayı) D5

This cistern is the grandest and most impressive one of its kind. The giant reservoir was built in the 6th century. The water that came from the Belgrade Forest 19km away, was used for the palaces. Its volumetric capacity was 80.000 cbm. It's 140m long and 70m wide. Its 336 columns, which support the brick dome, are arranged in 12 rows of 28 each and are topped by Byzantine Corinthian capitals. On the 8m-high columns one can still notice the marks left by the water level. This subterranean palace that hasn't been in use for centuries is a museum now. A few scenes from the James Bond film "Greetings from Moscow" were shot in the cistern.

Cistern of 1001 columns (Binbirdirek Sarnıcı) D5

This cistern is also located near the old Hippodrome and is known to be the second largest of the covered cisterns. It dates back to the 6th century. In the rectangular ground plan, 64m×56m, the 224 columns arranged in 16 rows of 14 each support the brick dome. (at the moment it can be visited with the permission of the authorities)

Head of medusa in the cistern

THE BAZAARS

THE EGYPTIAN BAZAAR (Spice Bazaar) (Mısır Çarşısı) C5

It was built in 1660 by Hatice Sultan with the taxes collected from Cairo for the trade of Egyptian commodities, especially herbs and spices. The domed bazaar is L-shaped and belongs to the complex of the Mosque of the Sultan's Mother (see page 69).

Despite the modern shops the Egyptian Bazaar and the neighbourhood have an oriental aura. The narrow streets around the bazaar with innumerable grocery stores, fish markets, and flower shops, convey an unforgettable atmosphere to the visitor.

Above the entrance gate is the famous first class Restaurant Pandelli serving Turkish dishes only at lunch time.

The Egyptian Bazaar

Spice shops by the Egyptian Bazaar

Spice shop in the Egyptian Bazaar

THE COVERED BAZAAR (Kapalı Çarşı) C5

In 1461 Sultan Mehmet II built the first bazaar of wood, - now called «Eski Bedesten»-the primitive cell. After several fires the bazaar was reconstructed in 1894 (the most recent fire broke out in 1954).

Today the domed building surrounded by a wall, occupies an area of 200.000 sq.m. Approximately 5000 stores spread out in a giant labyrinth, of small streets and passages, which are mostly arranged according to their trades: rugs, antiques, gold, silver, leather etc.

The visitor has to find his way out. He might have planned to take a stroll only; but he leaves the bazaar with full bags and an empty wallet - the bazaar is so interesting and the sales people are so skilful. To visit the bazaar is an adventure; you have to keep in mind that you have to be as skilful as the dealers while shopping.

Unfortunately, among the offered goods there is also a lot of junk. The hand-made merchandise is recommended. Because of the low cost of labour the prices of hand-woven Turkish carpets, gold and silver jewellery and leather clothing are moderate. Also, objects of copper, brass and onyx are offered as souvenirs.

If high quality is your first priority, there are fine export shops in Nuruosmaniye Street which accept credit cards and cheques. They insure your order, and post it to your country.

The Covered Bazaar

The Covered Bazaar

A carpet weaver

Turkish "Hereke" silk rugs

Turkish souvenirs

The land walls

THE CITY WALLS (Şehir Surları)

The Marble Tower

They exist of land walls and sea walls:

The land walls are 6.5 km long. They extend between the Marmara Sea (the Marble Tower) and the Golden Horn. The last piece on the Golden Horn was added in 1150 during the reign of Emperor Manuel II Comnenus to protect the Byzantine Palace of Blachernae.

There are no remains of the walls of Byzantium, built by Septimius Severus and Constantine the Great. The walls we see today were constructed during the reign of Theodosius II in 413.

The plan of the land walls built by Theodosius:

The inner walls, outer walls, parateichion and the moat.

The inner walls were 13m high, 3-4m thick and were guarded by 96 towers 15-20m high.

The outer walls were 8m high, approximately 2m thick and had 96 towers 15-20m high.

The moat was 18m wide and 7m deep. During a siege it was flooded with water.

The cross-section of the Theodosian walls

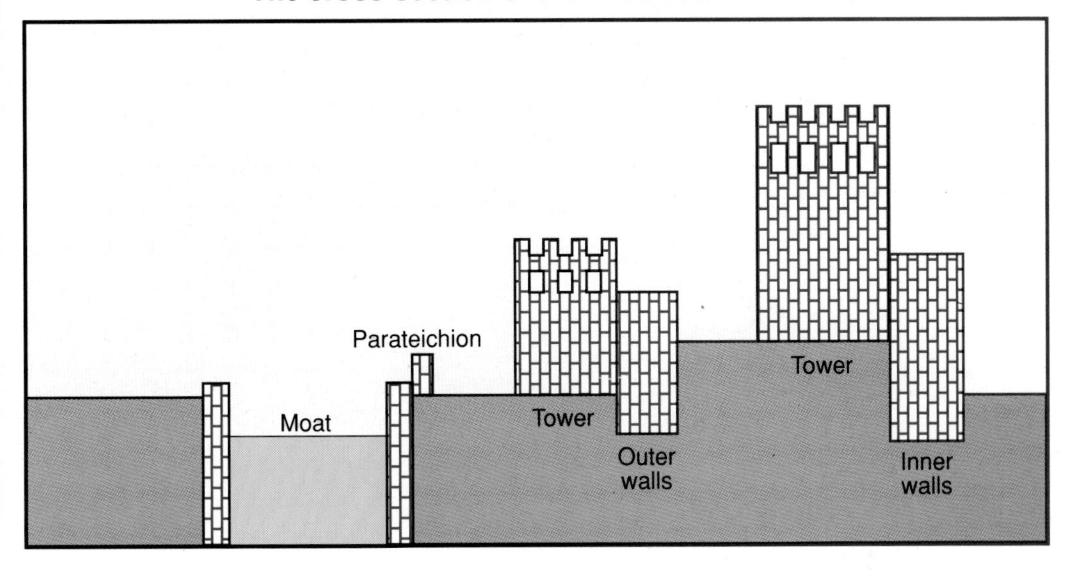

The defence wall consists of square blocks of lime-stones and layers of red brick. 10 gates lead into the city through the walls (see the city plan). The most important ones are as follows:

Edirnekapı (Gate of Hadrian)

Topkapı (Gate of Romanos); In 1453 the Turks entered the city through this gate.

Yedikule with the Golden Gate (see page 80)

The sea walls consist of a single row and include two parts:

1- The 9km-long wall along the Marmara Sea,
2- The 5km-long wall along the Golden Horn.

The wall along the Marmara Sea starts at Seraglio Point, the mouth of the Golden Horn, and links up with the land walls at the Marble Tower. It was 12-15m high and had 150 towers and 8 gates. Today its remains are to be seen here and there.

The wall along the Golden Horn was 5km long and 10m high. It had 100 towers and 14 gates.

Both rows of wall were built during the reign of Theodosius II in the 5th century.

The land walls

The "Yedikule" Citadel

The "Yedikule" Citadel (the Castle of the Seven Towers) A6

Yedikule is an interesting structure, partly Byzantine and partly Ottoman. The walls form a five-sided enclosure, which surrounds a big courtyard with the remains of a minaret in the centre. Here there was never a palace in the usual sense; it was a Roman triumphal arch erected in 390 by Theodosius I. This arch, once called the Golden Gate. had three gilded gates, the middle one of which was larger than the other two, and this difference is still seen although the gates have been walled up.

The old gate of Yedikule

Theodosius II enlarged the «Golden Gate» and added four towers. Today's citadel with seven towers, was completed when Sultan Mehmet II added three more towers following the conquest of the city in the 15th century. During Ottoman times, the citadel first served as the treasury and later as a prison.

To the right of the entrance is «the Tower of the Ambassadors». Envoys of foreign countries at war with the Ottoman Empire were imprisoned here. What these prisoners carved on the walls can still be read today.

The pylon to the left of the Golden Gate was used as a prison. Sultan Osman was executed here at the age of 17 in 1622.

The fountain of Ahmet III

The fountain of Emperor Wilhelm II

The Fountains (Sebil or Çeşme)

a selection

The Fountain of Ahmet III (Sultan Ahmet Çeşmesi) D5

This fountain is the most beautiful one of its kind in Istanbul, It was erected by Sultan Ahmet in rococo style in 1728. The square structure of marble with bronze-gilt alcoves has an overhanging roof surmounted by five small domes, one in the centre and the others at the four corners. Valuable tiles and fine inscriptions adorn this handsome fountain that stands in front of the main gate of Topkapı Place.

The Fountain of Emperor Wilhelm İI (Alman Çeşmesi) D5

This octangular marble structure was given by Emperor Wilhelm II to Sultan Abdülhamit II as a present to commemerate his visit to Istanbul in 1895 and was completed in 1898. It has polished granite columns and a gold mosaic dome with the insignia of the sultan and the emperor.

The gate of the University and Beyazıt Tower

The Beyazit Tower C5

In the centre of the university park, behind the monumental gate, stands this interesting tower from the year 1828. Before its construction there was a wooden tower at this site for fire-watchers. 180 wooden steps lead to the top from where you have a wonderful view. The tower now serves as a weather forecast station. The colours of the light bulbs located on the mast, indicate the weather for the next day (blue=nice weather, green=rain, yellow=fog and red=snow). Sometimes you can't see any colour then it means short-circuit!

The "Burnt Column"

The Burnt Column (Çemberlitaş) C5

This monument of Emperor Constantine stands in the centre of the Forum Constantine. It was erected in 328 A.D. and had the bronze-gilt statue of the emperor in the figure of Apollo, which was destroyed in stormy weather in the 12th century

It's called the "Burnt Column" because of its blackish colour, which may be the result of a fire.

To protect the column against earthquakes iron hoops were added. The shaft consists of six porphyry drums. Their rims are decorated with wreaths of laurel. The total height is 36m.

View of the Golden Horn from the Süleymaniye Mosque

THE GOLDEN HORN (Haliç)

The Golden Horn, an inlet of the sea, one of the natural harbours in the world, is located between the two European quarters of Istanbul (the old Istanbul and the modern Istanbul). Since antiquity, this arm of the Bosphorus has been called "Golden Horn" because of its form like a horn, and the golden colour of the water surface at sunset. It is 11km long, has an average depth of 40m, and its max. width reaches 800m.

Through centuries, pretty palaces and pavilions with large and well-maintained gardens were built along its banks. People who lived in Istanbul loved it as a holiday resort, where they could spend happy hours by the tree-shaded springs. Unfortunately, the Golden Horn has lost its romantic look because of the factories that pollute the water; however, it is pleasing to know that the new government plans to bring back the pleasant original look of the Golden Horn.

My description corresponds to the route of the ferries:

Ist station: **Haliç İskelesi** (in Eminönü)

It is located in front of the Egyptian Bazaar, 100m away from Galata Bridge. The 470m-long bridge was built by the Man company in 1912; it rests on 22 pontoons. During the trip, we see the Rüstem Pasha Mosque on the left-hand side in the foreground (see page 68). Behind it there are the Süleyman Mosque on the hill (see page 72) and the Aqueduct of Valens (see page 72), to the right Galata Tower (see page 90) dominates the whole hill. In the meantime, the ferry goes under the Atatürk Bridge and stops at the right bank.

2nd station: **Kasımpaşa** (on the right side)

This district takes its name from the mosque of Süleyman's grand vizier Güzelce Kasım. Probably this is the point were the Turks transported their ships on a wooden slide over the land and into the

Golden Horn. Later the Ottoman naval arsenal was built here. On the bank there is a pretty building from the 19th century, which was the residence of the admirals in charge.

3rd station: **Fener** (on the left side)

The name is deriven from the old Greek "phanar" (lighthouse). On the hill rises the beautiful Selim Mosque from the 16th century (see page 70). Farther down there is a building of brick from the 19th century; it houses the Greek Orthodox high school. Then we see the plain-looking church of the Greek Orthodox Patriarchate (Hagios Georgios), built in 1720. After the ferry anchors, right at the bank the church of St. Stephen of the Bulgars which is constructed of cast iron, comes into sight (1871).

4th station: **Balat** (on the left side)

Between this station and the next one (Hasköy) Mehmet II built a bridge over the Golden Horn in 1453.

5th station: **Hasköy** (on the right side)

On the right are dockyards, and above the houses there is a big Jewish cemetery, where the gravestones lie prone on the ground. To the left the "Tekfur Saray", the imperial residence of the late Byzantine Empire, stands on the hill. Below the palace, the ruins of the old city wall become visible. The ferry goes under the modern highway bridge (Haliç Köprüsü) of 1973 and stops at the last station.

6th station: **Eyüp** (on the left side)

The Eyüp Mosque with the tomb of the standard-bearer of the prophet stands approximately 200m behind the landing stage. On the sides of the hill behind the mosque, we see the old Islamic cemetery and the Cafe Pierre Loti which is on its peak (see page 86). Two km to the north of Eyüp, two streams called the Fresh Waters of Europe flow into the Golden Horn; once they were amongst the favourite holiday resorts in Istanbul.

Sunset on the Golden Horn

View of the Golden Horn from the Cafe Pierre Loti

Eyüp Mosque (Eyüp Sultan Camii) B2

It is the holiest mosque in the city. Especially for the Turkish Sunnite Moslems, the mosque follows the sacred places in Mecca, Medina and Jerusalem, because here lies Mohammed's standard-bearer "Eyüp Ensari", who was killed during the first siege of Istanbul by the Arabs (672-679).

Eight hundred years later, the Turks conquered the city under the command of Mehmet II in 1453 and discovered the burial site of the standard-bearer. To commemerate this discovery Mehmet II built a mosque and dedicated it to Eyüp. Murat III remodelled the mosque, and in 1800 Selim III reconstructed it completely. After the conquest of Istanbul by the Turks the Ottoman sultans were girded here with the sword of Osman (the founder of the Ottoman dynasty) on their accession to the throne, which is a ceremony equivalent to the coronation of European rulers.

The mosque has an outer courtyard with an ablution fountain. Here old storks and herons build their nests on the trees and hundreds of pigeons fly around.

The ground plan is a rectangle. The dome sits on a cylinder which rests on eight semi-domes. The domed hall is surrounded by a three-sided balcony. Behind a plane-tree opposite the main entrance of the mosque, is the türbe ('burial site) of **the standard-bearer of the prophet** (closed on Mondays). It is an octagonal structure enclosed by a vestibule on three sides. Everybody can visit the grave site; the only condition is that women wear a headcover. The inner and outer walls are revetted with fine tiles, which are the most beautiful examples of Iznik ceramics (16th-19th c.). The standard-bearer must have been buried in the middle of the octagonal building under a big and slightly elevated wooden sarcophagus which is covered with silver-embroidered velvet. A silver grid surrounds the sarcophagus. Two standards of the prophet are also kept here.

Often there are people praying in front of the "wish window" to plead for a solution to their problems. When the wish is fulfilled, it is customary to sacrifice a sheep or a rooster, and to distribute the meat among the needy. -For this purpose there is

Mosque of Eyüp

a sacrificial place nearby.

Also according to a tradition of ours, before circumcision, young boys in formal attire, visit the tomb with their parents hoping that the small operation will be carried out without any complication. For sanitary purposes, the Islamic religion demands that all young boys be circumcised.

Cafe Pierre Loti A2

After a steep climb of approximately twenty minutes through the old cemetery, we reach a small coffee house furnished in the old Turkish style. From here we can enjoy the wonderful view of the Golden Horn and Istanbul.

Pierre Loti (1850-1923) was a French lieutenant in the navy and an author, who was sent to Istanbul to teach the Turkish marines in the 19th century. As a friend of the Turks he wrote a lot of poems about Istanbul, the Golden Horn and life in the harem. During his stay in Istanbul he often came to this place.

Circumcision's boys

View of the Galata quarter with Galata Bridge

THE MODERN EUROPEAN CITY

The modern city, which occupies a large area, lies to the north of the Golden Horn. It has fewer sights to offer the visitor than the old "Stambul" (today's old city).

The Galata quarter , which was a Genoese settlement in the 13th century, lies to the south of Galata Tower, which also originates from that century. This old quarter forms a gigantic triangle with its corners comprising Galata Tower and the Atatürk and Galata Bridges. Today it is the quarter of whosale dealers, importers and old banks established in the last century.

The underground railway built in 1875 is the oldest one in all Europe. (see map D4). It is located in this quarter and connects the harbour section at Galata Bridge with İstiklâl Street . Today an electric train operates between the two stations 620m apart from each other.

The Beyoğlu quarter (the old Pera), lies to the north of Galata Tower. It stretches to the north with many business streets, consulates and banks. In the sixteenth century the first embassies moved here, and in the 19th century, foreign companies and banks were established. This area has been the heart of Istanbul for the last few centuries. In the last thirty years the business district has extended to the north, to the areas of Osmanbey and Şişli , where the most exclusive shops in Istanbul are located (see map D2). The most important street of the modern city is "İstiklal Caddesi" (Street of Independence) (see map D3). With its stores, restaurants and pubs, it is a busy street, alive both day and night. A few consulates and. cinemas are also located in this street. Istanbul's nightlife, can be found in the side streets.

Taksim Square and the Monument of Independance

The following restaurants are recommended for their belly-dancing and folk-dance shows.

Kervansaray (by the Hilton Hotel)
Taşlık Maksim (in the Maçka-Taşlık quarter)
Galata Tower (on the upper level), beautiful view!

At the end of «İstiklal Street» Taksim Square is located,This is the main square of the new town. The Monument of Independance created by the Italian sculptor «Canoni», in 1928, stands in the centre. On one side it depicts Atatürk in the decisive battle against the Greeks. On the other side Atatürk is with İsmet İnönü and Marshal Çakmak at the declaration of the republic (see map D3).

At the eastern side of the square, the new Opera House and the luxury hotel Etap Marmara are located. Nearby we see the other first-class hotels of the city: Sheraton and Hilton hotels. The open-air theatre, the sports hall and the technical university, are all in the same district.

Turkish belly dancer

Galata Tower

The Cannon Foundry

The Janissary Band in the Military Museum

Galata Tower D4

Today's tower was built by the Genoese colony at the site of the Tower of Christ (6th century) in 1348, to protect the "Galata" quarter. In 1446 upper levels were added and the tower was fortified. During Ottoman times, the tower was used as a prison and as a fire-watch tower.

Since 1975 it has had a new roof built to the original design. It is 68m high and has nine storeys. The balcony, from where the view of the city is magnificent, is 140m above sea-level. On the upper levels, there are now a fine restaurant that offers an Oriental atmosphere, a Turkish cafe and a Genoese tavern.

The bridge of the sultan's galley inlaid with mother-of-pearl in the Naval Museum

The Military Museum (Askeri Müze) D2

This interesting museum is located a few hundred metres away from the Hilton Hotel, and was founded in 1959 and housed in the former Military Academy. The following pieces from the 12th-20th centuries are exhibited: weapons, helmets, spears, armour, bows, arrows, tents, Janissaries uniforms and a part of the chain which was used to drag ships over the land to the Golden Horn during the siege of Istanbul. Documents of the Turkish War of Independance, medals, and weapons from the Korean War are also displayed in the museum.

Every day at 3:00 p.m. the Janissairies Band, dressedd in traditional costumes, plays old military music, which is an interesting event to see.

Earlier Turkish marines in the Naval Museum

The Naval Museum (Deniz Müzesi) E3

Today's museum was founded in 1961. The development of the Turkish naval forces since the foundation of the Ottoman Empire can be traced here. Important exhibits are:

The map of America, drawn in 1513 by the Turkish admiral «Piri Reis», which author Erich von Däniken mentions in one of his books, caiques of the sultans ship models, fire-arms, portraits of famous captains and Atatürk's cabin from his yacht «Ertuğrul».

In the garden cannons and equipment from the old war ships are exhibited.

Dolmabahçe Mosque

Dolmabahçe Mosque (Dolmabahçe Camii) E3

This mosque built by the mother of Sultan Abdülmecit «Bezmi Alem» is located on the European shore of the Bosphorus. It was constructed in 1853 in baroque and renaissance styles.

The ground plan is a square. The large dome sits on a cylinder, which is supported by the outer walls of the mosque. In each corner is a small tower. The mihrab and the mimber of red porphyry are interesting. The two minarets are the most slender ones in Istanbul.

Victory Mosque (Nusretiye Camii) D4

Here there was a mosque from the end of the 18th century for the soldiers who, were quartered at this site. In 1823 Sultan Mahmut II built the new mosque which is decorated with baroque and empire motives at the same place. It's a single-dome mosque and is flanked by two slender minarets with two galleries each. Today it is located at the goods-harbour of Istanbul. An ablution fountain, water fountain and a room of clocks belong to the complex.

Kılıç Ali Pasha Mosque (Kılıç Ali Paşa Camii) D4

It was donated by Admiral Kılıç Ali Pasha and built by the architect Sinan in 1580, on the shore of the Bosphorus. The designs of the domes and the structure of the high side walls, remind us of Haghia Sophia.

The tiles in the inner hall, especially on the mihrab, have been arranged artistically. The lunettes with stained glass are also noteworthy.

In the garden of the mosque are the türbe (tomb) of the donor and an old Turkish bath.

Cannon Foundry (Tophane) D4

This ancient building dates back from the conquest of Istanbul. Today's monumental structure with several domes and towers originates from the year 1803. Currently, it's used as a military depot and is inaccessible.

Dolmabahçe Palace

PALACES ALONG THE BOSPHORUS

Dolmabahçe Palace (Dolmabahçe Sarayı) E3

Dolmabahçe means 'filled garden' and refers to the small harbour, which Sultan Ahmet I filled in to build his pleasure palace. After several fires Sultan Abdülmecit I, who found the old Topkapı Palace old-fashioned, erected the present palace in the Turkish Renaissance style at the same site in 1843-1856. It served as the official residence of the sultans till 1876. In 1877 Sultan Abdülhamit II opened the first Turkish parliament here, which was dissolved two months later. Among other celebrities the French Empress Eugenie, wife of Napoleon III, the Austrian Emperor Franz Josef, the German Emperor Wilhelm II, the English Prince Edward VIII, the Persian Shah Reza Pahlewi, King Faisal of Iraq and King Emanullah of Afghanistan, were guests here. The palace is still the scene of important official receptions.

After the empire was terminated in 1923 Atatürk stayed at the palace on his trips to Istanbul. He died here on November 10th 1938 at the age of 57.

The palace built according to the plans of the architect "Balian" consists of three parts (with our back to the Bosphorus): the official building is on the left, the throne hall is in the centre and the harem is on the right. The 285 rooms and 43 halls, house 280 vases, 156 clocks, 58 crystal candlesticks and 36 chandeliers of Bohemian, Venetian, French and English crystal. 4,500 sq.m. of handwoven silk "Hereke carpets" cover the marvellous parquet floors of the rooms. The curtains and the upholstery are also made of silk Hereke fabric. The palace has 6 balconies and 6 baths.

To furnish the interior and decorate the rooms, 14 tons of gold and 40 tons of silver were used. The construction of the palace cost 5 million gold coins, which is now the equivalent of about 500 million US dollars.

A visit to the palace:

The harem and a few rooms in the official section of the palace aren't accessible. Hoping that the closed parts will be open to the public soon, I'll describe most of the palace. Through a magnificent gate we enter a big and well-maintained garden of selected trees. A fountain decorated with swans embellishes the centre of the garden.

The Reception Hall: This is the first room we enter. Here, the ambassadors were initially received. In the middle of the hall hangs a chandelier of French "baccarat" crystal, one of 36 similar chandeliers in the palace. Tiled heating-stoves with small crystal bars hanging over them stand in the corners. They were made in the "Yıldız" factory.When the sun shines on the crystal bars, you can see the seven colours of the rainbow on the parquet floor. On both sides of the hall there are two rooms each with the same decoration.

The Staircase Hall: Here a big crystal chandelier hangs in the centre. Since the roof is made of glass, this is the most luminous room in the whole palace. The symmetric staircase is of great attraction. The pretty crystal bannisters are made of Venetian glass. Two beautiful Sevres vases stand on both side of the staircase. Upstairs in front of the Spanish wall, two silver oil lamps sent to the sultan by the governor of Hedjaz hang on a pair of elephant tusks.

The Hall of the Ambassadors: (Mabeyn Salonu) This hall which has a magnificent ceiling decoration, was used to receive the ambassadors officially. The golden wood-carved ceiling is the work of Italian and French artists. A 110 sq.m. silk carpet made in the royal factory of Hereke is placed under the French crystal chandelier. The bearskins on the floor were sent by the Russian Czar Nicholas II. To the west of the hall is a big silver instrument with a clock, a barometer and a thermometer inside, also a gift from the governor of Hedjaz.

Farther to the right there are two rooms one after the other.

The Waiting-Room of the Interpreters: Is the smaller one of the two. A few valuable paintings by the Russian artist "Aiwazowsky", who lived in the palace for some time, decorate the walls. The neighbouring room is:

The baroque clock tower in front of the palace

The magnificent gate of the palace

The First Waiting-Room of the Ambassadors: After the official reception, the ambassadors and their staff waited here. On each side of the entrance of this room there are two beautiful fireplaces of crystal with big mirrors over them.

Through the Hall of the Ambassadors we reach the rooms nearest the seashore.The first of them is:

The Second Waiting-Room of the Ambassadors: The ambassadors waited here alone to be taken to the sultan for a private audience.

The Red Room: In the back is the bigger room, where the sultan had confidential talks with the ambassadors. Walls with mahogany panels, red silk fabrics and golden curtain rods give the room a special character. In the corners there are four small round enamel tables, which were gifts from Napoleon III, sent to the sultan and his wife. The one on the right side has the portrait of Napoleon Bonaparte in the centre and portraits of his relatives on the sides.

The Panorama Hall: Walking through the Hall of the Ambassadors and the Staircase Hall we come to the Panorama Hall, where religious holidays and weddings were celebrated. There are two attractive mother-of-pearl inlaid cabinets from Damascus.

The gardens of the palace

The Staircase Hall

Music Room: Here we see a harpsichord and other musical instruments belonging to Sultan Abdülmecit.

The marble Bathroom Suite of the sultan: It consists of three parts: a lounge, a dressing room and a bathroom with a large terrace in the front. The walls of the last two rooms, are sheathed with alabaster panels from Egypt. The sultan's oval bathtub and the basin, are each made from a block of alabaster.

The Gallery of Paintings: Is located right next to the bathroom suite, and houses portraits of rulers such as Emperor Wilhelm I and Emperor Franz Josef and statuettes of Queen Victoria and a few Ottoman sultans. A long corridor decorated with paintings and vases leads to the harem. It was only used by women. Through the barred windows they watched the celebrations in the Throne Hall.

The Blue Hall (The Banquet Hall of the Harem)

Behind the iron gate, which separates the harem and the men's section, there is another corridor, the walls of which are decorated with the paintings of "Zonaro" and "Guillement", the artists of the palace. From here we proceed to the apartment of the sultan's mother.

*** The reception room of the sultan's mother:** has a gilt-decorated fireplace of white marble. A Gobelin carpet is placed on the floor. There is a Sevres vase on the black gilt table in the centre. With the fascinating domed ceiling and the red satin upholstery the room looks very charming.

*** The bedroom of the sultan's mother:** In this room the gilt baldachino bed, the closet and the beautiful jewellery box(made in the Yıldız factory) inlaid with mother-of-pearl are noteworthy.

*** The Blue Hall:**(the Banquet Hall of the harem) All kinds of ceremonies took place in this hall, which is richly decorated in blue. It was also used for the enthroning of the sultans. A valuable red and white chandelier hangs on the gilt-carved ceiling.

*** Atatürk's study:** Before Atatürk, the last sultans used the room as the winter room. The adjacent room is

*** Atatürk's death room:** Atatürk (Father of Turks) died here on November 10th 1938 at the age of 57.

*Inaccessible rooms

The Yellow Hall (The Meeting Hall of the Harem Ladies)

The Throne or the Banquet Hall

*** The Yellow Hall:** (the meeting hall of the harem ladies) The hall takes its name from the richly-used gold colour on the mirrors, consoles and the upholstery. For a long time Atatürk used the room as his lounge. From here we enter

*** The bedrooms of the sultan's wives:** The bedroom of the first lady has a walnut gilt-carved bed and an interesting tiled heating-stove. The bedroom of the second wife, which is dominated by red, has a bronze-decorated bed, and the bedroom of the third wife is decorated and furnished in white. It's interesting to compare the quality of the fixtures in these rooms.

*** The bedroom of Sultan Reşat:** This is the last room in the harem on the first floor by the sea. There is a beautiful baldachino bed made of mahogany and walnut. The artistic joinery of the furniture in this room is noteworthy.

*** The Harem Bath Suite:** This suite, which consists of a lounge, a dressing room and a toilet, is located behind the Yellow Hall on the inland side of the palace and is revetted with marble plates as well as tiles. This tiled heating stove in the lounge is very attractive. After passing dark passages, we enter...

***Inaccessible rooms**

* **The bedroom of Sultan Abdülaziz:**The elaborate oversize bed of the sultan, who weighed 150 kg, is on the right in the corner,Looking farther to the left we see two gilt vases.

After walking through the Blue Hall and down the stairs, we come to

* **The bedroom of Sultan Abdülmecit:** (the founder of the palace) There is a valuable silver-plated baldachino bed inlaid with mother-of-pearl. Two Sevres vases on the table have the sultan's sıgnature called "Tuğra". A colourful crystal chandelier dominates this room.

The Throne Hall: is the largest and most magnificent room of the whole palace with dimensions of 44m×46m. 56 columns stand on all sides. The richly-painted dome is 36m high and below we see a mezzanine reserved for guests, dignitaries and the orchestra. The 4.5 ton chandelier with 750 lamps, all in the form of a candle, was a gift from Queen Victoria of England. It is one of the biggest chandeliers in the world. The openings under the columns are evidence of the old floor heating system of the palace. The central heating was installed later, during the reign of Sultan Abdülhamit II at the turn of the century.

The coronation of the last five sultans took place in this hall, where the 250kg"Bayram Throne" was placed each time. (Today it is exhibited in the treasury of Topkapı Palace.)

After Atatürk died, the body of this extraordinary leader was kept here, where his epigraph can be read on a big board. Old generals stood on guard of honour with drawn swords at his bedside, while torches flared.

* **The Hall of Maps:** At the staircase leading to the first floor hangs a big map, on which the expansion of the Ottoman Empire is shown.

* **The Mosque:** There are two connected rooms on the inland side. The first room is the prayer room, with a niche and a gilt-enamelled pulpit. The second room was designed for reading the Koran.

* **The Departure Hall:** The hall, with a large silk Hereke carpet in the centre is supported by columns. The room has illusory arches on the walls, and a beatifully painted ceiling.

* **The office:** The tiled room, is decorated with Chinese vases. On the corridor to the secretary's office, hangs a giant painting with a golden frame on the wall. It depicts a caravan on the way to Macca.

*Inaccessible rooms

The dome of the Throne Hall

Beylerbeyi Palace

Beylerbeyi Palace (Beylerbeyi Sarayı) G3

This palace constructed in the same style as the Dolmabahçe Palace is located on the Asiatic shore of the Bosphorus. It was built during the reign of Sultan Abdülaziz by the architect "Balian" in the year 1865. It is a long, rectangular and double-storeyed palace with two marble pavilions at each end of the quay; beautiful gardens border the pavilions. It looks like the European pleasure palaces of the late 18th century, and is decorated with ornaments in the Oriental baroque form with classic motives.

The palace consists of 24 rooms and 6 halls. Italian, French and Turkish artists created the ceiling decorations. Aside from decorative purposes, the Venetian crystal mirrors also have the task of strengthening the candlelight to make the rooms look more spacious. In the corners there are paintings of ships made by the Russian artist Aywazowsky. Beylerbeyi Palace has no heating system because it's a summer palace. The bronze-gilt doors are made of mahogany, walnut and oak. The attractive door knobs were manufactured in the Yıldız factory in Istanbul

The building consists of three parts: (seen from the sea) the harem is located on the left, the men's section (selamlık) is on the right, and each floor has a big hall in the centre. In the middle of the lower hall there's an interesting marble basin.

The sultans used to put their guests up in this palace. The Emperor Franz Josef of Austria, King Edward VIII of England and the Shah Nasireddin of Persia, were accomodated here during their stay in Istanbul.

When Sultan Abdülhamit II returned from exile at Salonica, he lived in the palace, where he later died in 1918.

A visit to the palace:

Walking through the northern garden on the seaward side of the palace, we come to the main entrance. The first room we enter is the **Entrance Hall** with a Bohemian crystal chandelier in the middle. The floors of the palace are covered with straw mats from Egypt, to protect the palace against humidity. The staircase leading to the first floor is opposite the entrance. Two big Japanese vases are placed on the last stair, and there is a beautiful Sevres vase on the table in the centre.

The Entrance Hall

We go to the left side and see three adjacent rooms before us. The room on the left was used as **the secretary's office.** The one next to it was **the waiting room for visitors.** On the parquet floor stands a mahogany table with a beautiful vase that draws our attention. The third room served as **the reception room of the Minister of Naval Affairs**, where the bronze-gilt arms and legs of the furniture show rope forms. Beautiful paintings by "Şeker Ahmet Paşa" hang on the wall, and paintings of ships adorn the ceiling.

After we leave the reception room, we enter the magnificent hall with a marble basin in the centre, where various celebrations took place. Each corner of the basin has a big Chinese vase. Farther to the left we see the **Reception Hall of the Sultan.** The backs of the chairs are set at right angles, because visitors had to sit upright in the presence of the sultan. The bronze-gilt curtain rod carved from a single wood block is very interesting.

Right behind the Reception Hall, the harem of the palace is located. The first thing we see here is the giant closet, where beds for the guests used to be stored. To the left of the closet is **the dining room of the sultan's mother,** in the centre of which stands a long table for 20 guests. All the chairs upholstered with antelope skin were carved by Sultan Abdülhamit II, carving was his hobby. His signature is inlaid in ivory on the backs of the chairs. Four buffets and historical paintings adorn this room.

We turn right and see the large **Entrance Chamber of the Harem** in front of us. The main entrance to the harem is on the left, and on the right the staircase leads to the first floor. We pass the stairs and come to **the bedroom of the first wife of Abdülhamit II.** The adjacent room is the bedroom of Abdülhamit II, where he spent his last years after he came back from exile at Salonica, and died after 33 years on the throne. To avoid the splendour of the buildings he must have purposely chosen this room overlooking the garden. We return to the Entrance Chamber of the Harem, walk up the stairs and come to the beautiful **Meeting Hall of Women,** which is also called the Hall of Mother-of-Pearl because of the rich mother-of-pearl inlays of the furniture. A big table, with a vase of "Yıldız porcelain" stands in the centre of the hall. On both sides of the table in front of the wall, we see two magnificent cabinets inlaid with mother-of-pearl.

To the left we see an attractive Italian cabinet, and to the right is the cabinet in which Sultan Abdülaziz kept his hunting guns. Both sides of the staircase are decorated with jewellery cabinets containing several drawers, which could be opened by hidden knobs.

We continue our walk on the right side. To our right is the bathroom. Opposite the bathroom, is **the bedroom for foreign guests.** The adjacent room, the furniture of which was brought from Yıldız Palace was **the study of Sultan Abdülhamit II.** To the right two bookcases are placed, and between them is a bureau.

We trace our steps back through the Hall of Mother-of-Pearl, and come to the seaward side, where three neighbouring rooms are located. The first one to the right was **the harem bath.** The painting "Horse Carriage" done by Prince Edward hangs in the second room, which was used by the sultan's mother as her **recepcion room.** After visiting this room, we leave the harem and enter the **Blue Hall,** which was built in German baroque style and is surrounded by big arcades. In the center of the hall is a 60 kg clock (gift of the Russian Czar Nicholas II) on the enamel table, over which hangs a big crystal chandelier of Istanbul.The other four crystal chandeliers are of Bohemian origin. The pure Hereke silk carpet covers 150sq.m. in the centre of the hall. Both glass cases at the western wall contain the first products of the "Yıldız Porcelain Factory", among which are the water pitcher, and the Turkish coffee cup of Atatürk. One room is located at each of the corners of the Blue Hall:

The first room on the seaward side was **the sultan's study.** It has a beautiful ceiling and the vases in the room are Japanese. The second room, one of the most beautiful rooms in the palace, was **the reception room of Sultan Abdülaziz** (he weighed 150 kg), whose big bronze-gilt chair of state is displayed here. The third room in the rear was **"Eugenie"s bedroom,** with the bath and rest room. The fourth room was **the wedding room.**

Upon leaving the Blue Hall, we enter **the conference room of Sultan Abdüzaliz.** The beauty of this room is beyond imagination. The walls and floor are covered with panels of walnut. The four carved niches in the wall draw our attention.

Next to it, is **the sultan's prayer room**. Then we turn right and see **the Hall of Mother-of Pearl (the Meeting Hall),** the furniture of which is decorated with mother-of-pearl. We walk through this wonderful hall and enter **the lounge,** used by the sultan to rest after meals. This room and the dining-room,are decorated with panels of walnut. At the long table we see 25 chairs also upholstered by Sultan Abdülhamit II in antelope skin.

We walk down the stairs and leave the palace through the Entrance Hall.

The Audience Chamber

The Blue Hall

The Palace of Çırağan which has been restored (1992)

Küçüksu Palace (Küçüksu Kasrı)

This pretty palace built in rococo style is on the asiatic shore of the Bosphorus, where one of the two Fresh Waters of Asia "Küçüksu" (a little stream) flows into the Bosphorus. Sultan Abdülmecit built it as his summer palace in 1856. The palace consists of two storeys, having a hall in the middle and four tastefully furnished rooms at the corners. The furniture in the palace and the walls of the building, resemble the other palaces along the Bosphorus.

During summertime Atatürk lived in one of the rooms on the first floor for a short time.

The beautiful baroque fountain of the sultan's mother "Mihrişah" from the year 1789, is located next to the palace.

Küçüksu Palace and the Bosphorus

Küçüksu Palace

Yıldız Palace and Yıldız Park F2

Exactly translated into English, the palace is called "the Star Palace" and was built during the second half of the 19th century by Sultan Abdülhamit, in the old style of the Ottoman residences.

Sultan Abdülhamit II was a despot, and ruled 33 years. Out of fear of an attempted assassination, he had strong walls built around the palace and 14.000 soldiers were stationed there to protect the him. Sultan Abdülhamit II lived in the palace until 1909: then the Young Turks dethroned him, and he died in Beylerbeyi Palace after returning from exile in Salonica.

The beautiful park of the palace is on the slopes of the Bosphorus behind the burnt-out "Çırağan Palace". The main building of the palace (which is inaccessible) and many other small pavilions scattered in the park, make up the palace complex. Today the renovated pavilions Malta Köşkü, Çadır Köşkü and the recently built Green and Pink Pavilions, are exclusive cafes which convey the Ottoman atmosphere of the 19th century to the visitor. Those who stay longer in Istanbul are advised to plan an excursion to the park.

The biggest pavilion in the area is the "Şale Köşk", which is only used for state receptions.

Çırağan Palace (Çırağan Sarayı) F3

This palace is on the European side of the Bosphorus below "Yıldız Park". It was built by Sultan Abdülaziz in 1863-1867; shortly after his overthrow he died here (1876). Sultan Abdülhamit II imprisoned Sultan Murat (who was dethroned in 1876) in the palace for 27 years.

In 1910 the palace burned out completely. In between the years of 1886-1990 it was restored and today it was converted into a five star hotel under the management of Kempinski group.

The "Malta Köşk" a pleasure pavilion

The Pink Pavilion

The Castle of "Rumeli Hisarı"

CASTLES ALONG THE BOSPHORUS

Rumeli Hisarı (the castle on the European shore of the Bosphorus)

Sultan Mehmet II the Conqueror erected this castle in 1452 on the European shore of the Bosphorus at its narrowest point. 10.000 men, 1.000 masons and lime-burners completed the construction in four months. It's known that high officials also helped with the construction.

The purpose was to control the strait so that Byzantine Istanbul could not receive aid from the Genoese trading centres at the Crimea during the siege by the Turks.

A strong wall surrounds the whole fortification, which has 3 big towers and 13 smaller ones. The three big towers were the winter headquarters of the janissaries. In summer the soldiers lived in tents, set up in the garden of the fortress. Today an open-air stage, at the site of which the mosque of the janissaries once stood, is located in the centre of the castle. In front of the entrance gate, cannons that could reach passing ships were placed.

In 1953 the castle was restored, in connection with the celebration of the five hundredth anniversary of the Conquest and inaugurated as a museum. During the summertime various theatrical events take place here.

Anadolu Hisarı (the castle on the Asiatic shore of the Bosphorus)

This small fortification is at the mouth of the stream "Göksu" (the Sky Stream) and was built by Sultan Beyazit I at the end of 14th century. In those

The castle of "Anadolu Hisarı"

"Göksu"-stream on the Asiatic side

days this castle was the only Turkish structure near Istanbul. Mehmet II (the Conqueror) extended the castle in 1452 and along with Rumeli Hisarı it blocked the Bosphorus. After the conquest of the city, the castle lost its importance. It was restored just a few years ago. It is a central structure with a big tower, which is surrounded by an inner wall and an outer circular wall.

THE BOSPHORUS AND THE PRINCES' ISLANDS

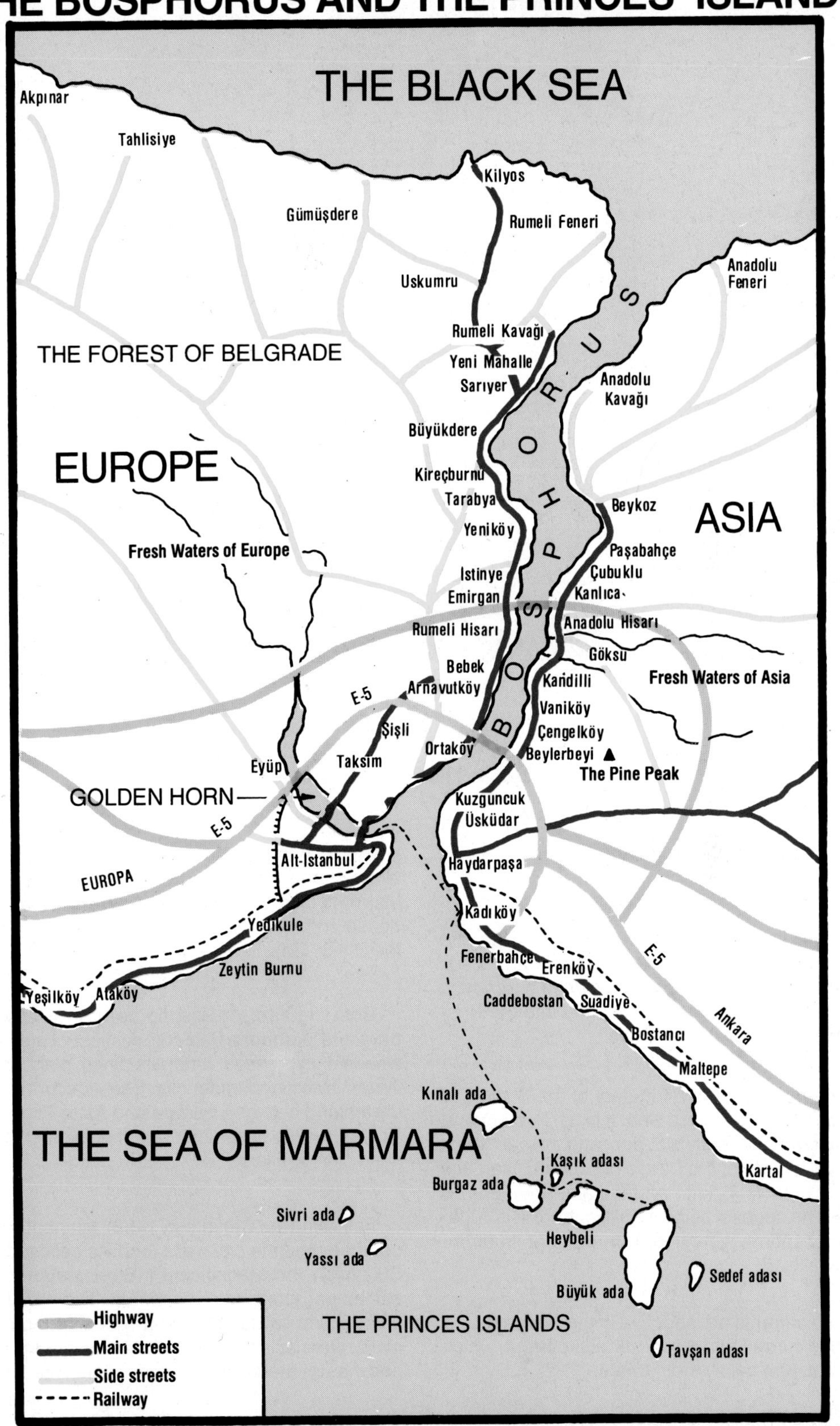

View of the Bosphorus

THE BOSPHORUS (Boğaziçi)

The word Bosphorus means "Ford of the Cow" and takes its name from a myth:

Io was the favourite of Zeus, but Hera, the wife of Zeus was jealous of her. To protect Io Zeus turned her into a cow, but Hera sent a bee, which irritated the cow, so that it plunged into the Bosphorus and crossed the strait.

The Bosphorus is a tributary of the Black Sea leading to the Marmara Sea. It is 31.7km long. At Büyükdere, the width is 3.3km, and the narrowest point is (660m) at the Castle of Rumeli Hisarı, the widest point is 4.7km., and the average depth is 70m. The deepest point is at Akıntıburnu (in Arnavutköy, 100m), where the current is at its strongest.

Two currents are effective in the Bosphorus: a surface current and a sub-surface current, which flows at 40m below the surface.

Through the surface current the waters flow at a rate of 3-4km per hour from the Black Sea to the Marmara Sea, and the lower current moves the dense and more saline waters of the Marmara to the Black Sea.

Both shores of the Bosphorus are indented with bays and harbours. Palaces, castles, villages and woods of cypresses, umbrella pines, plane trees, Judas trees and magnolia trees decorate this dreamland between Europe and Asia. Today the Bosphorus is the summer resort of over ten thousand city dwellers.

Following the Conquest (1453), Istanbul developed beyond the city walls, and it's believed that Süleyman the Magnificent (16th c.) started the settlement along the Bosphorus. The mosques, and the first yalıs (summer palaces of high officials), were built then. In the 17th century the yalıs and the summer palaces of the sultans, reached to

The Bosphorus Bridge

The new "Fatih Sultan Mehmet" bridge

The "Ortaköy" Mosque

the north along both shores. The buildings, which embellished the shores like a pearl necklace until the 19th century, were constructed of wood, and the architecture and decorations were influenced by the rococo style. With the nineteenth century a different era started, as more and more people settled along the Bosphorus. In the middle of the century, splendid palaces like Dolmabahçe, Beylerbeyi and Küçüksu were constructed in the European style. Till recently, real estate speculation threatened the whole Bosphorus area, the beauty of the shores and the existence of the remaining "yalıs". In the meantime a powerful special law was passed to put the Bosphorus and its valuable buildings under protection.

Now we want to explore the Bosphorus. My description won't follow the route of the ferries, which flit back and forth between the two shores. We'll assume that we are sailing along the European shore in the direction of the Black Sea and will cover the same distance on our way back along the Asiatic shore.

The European shore of the Bosphorus: According to my route, the ferry departs from the landing stage No. 4 at Gâlata Bridge and sailing past the gorgeous Dolmabahçe Palace stops at the first station.

Beşiktaş (cradle stone) is the name of the first district. The Naval Museum (see p.90) is located behind the ferry-landing.In the park next to the museum, is the statue of the Turkish Admiral «Barbaros Hayrettin Paşa», who lived in the 16th century. In 1946, the statue was erected on the 400th day of his death.

Farther to the left we see the burnt-out Çırağan Palace (see page 104), which was built in 1864 and gutted by fire in 1910. On the hill behind the palace is Yıldız Park (Park of stars), with a palace and a pleasure pavilion (see page 104).

Ortaköy (middle village) is the second stop on the European shore.It is situated just before the Bosphorus Bridge. The pretty 19th century «Ortaköy Mosque» stands on the shore before the bridge pylons.Then we sail under this suspension-bridge over the Bosphorus.On 29th October 1973 it was dedicated to the 50th anniversary of the Turkish Republic. The bridge constructed by the German firm "Hoch-Tief" and the British firm "Cleveland-Bridge" and was completed in three and a half years, is 1074m long between both pylons, and its total length is 1560m, the pylons themselves are 165m high. The roadway is 64m above water level, and 33.40m wide, taking six lanes of traffic. It's the second longest suspension-bridge in Europe, and the fifth longest one in the world, after the Humper Bridge in England, the Verrazano-Narrows in New York, the Golden Gate Bridge in San Francisco and the Mackinac Bridge in Michigan.

Approximately 200.000 vehicles cross the bridge every day, and it has paid for itself three times over. Because of the havy traffic on the bridge in 1988 was built the second suspension bridge called "Fatih Sultan Mehmet" over the Bosphorus.

Kuruçeşme is unfortunately the only ugly village with heaps of sand and coal lying on the shore, but the authorities have planned to restore this area in the near future.

Arnavutköy (the Albanian village) was earlier inhabited by the Albanians. It has a picturesque harbour with old villas along the shore. The deepest part of the Bosphorus (100m) is off the point of Arnavutköy.

Bebek with its rolling hills, is located on the bay of the same name. Right on the water's edge, is the Egyptian Embassy. Today, Bebek is one of the most affluent neighbourhoods of Istanbul. Bosphorus University stands on its northern hill.

Rumeli Hisarı is the most beautiful area on the Bosphorus. The narrowest point of 660m, is between the two old Turkish castles, which are situated facing each other. On the European side we see the great "Rumeli Hisarı", the citadel of the mid-15th century (see page 105), and the small and old "Anadolu Hisarı" of the 14th century (see page 105) stands on the Asiatic side. In 512 B.C. the Persian King Darius I chose to constructa bridge of boats at this site, where he led an army of 700.000 men against the Scythians. In 1097 the crusaders crossed the strait at this point, and so did the Turks in 1453.

Tarabya village on the European Side

Arnavutköy village on the European Side

Rumeli Kavağı, a fishing village on the European Side

We now sail under the new bridge "Fatih Sultan Mehmet". The bridge was constructed by a joint venture of Turkish, Japanese and Italian firms, and was dedicated on July 3rd 1988 after 26 months of labour. The roadway is 64m above sea-level and is 39m wide, taking 8 lines of traffic. This bridge is 1.050m long between the two pylons, and its total length is 1.510m, the pylons themselves are 106m high. It is the sixth biggest bridge of the world and came up to 120 million US dollars.

Baltalimanı (the axe harbour) is named after the admiral of Mehmet II. Here the admiral built the galleys, which were dragged over land to the Golden Horn.

Emirgan takes its name from the Persian «Emir Khan», who lived here in internment after surrendering to Sultan Murat IV in the 17th century. City-dwellers visit this town to enjoy the famous Turkish tea prepared in samovars in the tea gardens, which are shaded by plane trees. The town also has a park with a tulip garden. Every year at the end of April, a beautiful festival is held here.

Istinye According to a legend, the Argonauts erected a temple here. Later, Constantine the Great built a cloister at the same site. Today, the bay is filled with floating docks used for the maintenance of large ships. It's nice to know that they will be transferred soon to the shore of the Marmara Sea.

Yeniköy (the new village) is a popular excursion town, with beautiful villas and gardens. The long row of old summer embassies starts here. The tastefully furnished «Yalı of Sait Halim Paşa» is located next to the Hotel Carlton by the sea. It is from the 19th century, and belonged to one of the last grand viziers of the Ottoman empire.

Tarabya Its name is the modified form of «Therapia», which means cure. It is located on the bay of the same name. The German summer embassy stands on the southern shore. Sultan Abdülhamit gave this land to Emperor Wilhelm II as a gift. There are many seafood restaurants along the waterfront. The modern Hotel Tarabya is located to the north of the bay, which is full of sailing boats most of the time.

Büyükdere (the big brook), is a popular summer resort. The Bosphorus is 3.3km wide at this point. There are Russian and Spanish summer embassies here. From here, a road leads us inland to the «Belgrade Forest» 10km away. It is the only forest in European Istanbul. Once there was a village there with the same name. After the conquest of Belgrade (1521), Süleyman the Magnificent brought the villagers here to maintain the reservoirs and aqueducts feeding the cisterns of the city. We have the first view of the Black Sea from this town.

Sarıyer: Along the Bosphorus this is the largest village and has a very interesting fish market. Here the Museum of "Sadberk Koç Hanım" is noteworthy. It is an old yellow frame house, where a rich collection of crystal, porcelain and silverware is exhibited.

Rumeli Kavağı: This fisherman's village, where you can eat fresh fish at low prices, is located 2km after Sarıyer. This is the last stop of the ferry, and the public road ends here, the military road is closed to the public.

Rumeli Feneri (the European lighthouse) is the last village along the European shore of the Bosphorus. At the mouth of the Bosphorus, there are bare, dark and steep islets, which Jason and his Argonauts sailed past on their way to Colchis, in quest of the Golden Fleece. Every time a ship sailed to the Black Sea between the rocks, it risked smashing its hull. The brave Argonauts overcame the passage with Athena's help.

The Asiatic shore of the Bosphorus (Return trip to Istanbul).

Anadolu Feneri (the Asian lighthouse) is the last village along the Asiatic shore of the Bosphorus.

Anadolu Kavağı is the last ferry stop. It's a typical fisherman's village, where a 14th century Genoese palace of Byzantine origin dominates the view.

Hünkar İskelesi, where the sultans once had their summer palaces, gave its name to the treaty signed here in 1833 between the Ottoman Empire and Russia, to keep the warships off the Dardanelles.

Beykoz is located to the north of the bay of the same name, where in 1854 the Anglo-French fleet rode at anchor before the attack at the Crimea. In the background, the 200m-high Joshua hill (Yuşa Tepesi) dominates the whole area.

Paşabahçe (the Pasha's Garden) is located in the centre of the Bay of Beykoz, on the shore of which we see the ruins of the Persian-style palace of Murat III (16th c.). Today it is an industrial area with a glass factory and an alcohol distillery.

Çubuklu is on the southern shore of the same bay. In Byzantine times there was a famous «Cloister of the Unsleeping» built by Alexander the Great, where the monks prayed day and night. On a hill is the summer residence of the Viceroy of Egypt «Abbas Hilmi Paşa».

Kanlıca has been very famous for its yoghurt for centuries. Along the shore there are two yalıs (summer houses) which belonged to «Saffet Paşa» in the 18th century and «Amcazade Hüseyin Paşa», a former grand vizier. The second yali, the front part of which rests on piers above the water, was built In 1698 and is the oldest wooden building on the Bosphorus.

Anadolu Hisarı: (the Castle of Asia) Here the two Fersh Waters of Asia flow into the Bosphorus; «Göksu» (Sky Stream) and «Küçüksu» Little Stream) are 200m away from each other. The small Turkish castle «Anadolu Hisarı» built in 1398 (see p. 105) stands at the mouth of «Göksu». A meadow, on which the «Palace of Küçüksu» of the 19th century was built (the summer residence of Sultan Abdülmecit I), stretches between the streams. The elaborate fountain of the palace is noteworthy. (see page 103)

Kandilli: Here we see some more old summer houses, among which the «Yalı of Count Ostrolog» built in 1790'is the best preserved yalı. On the hill above Kandilli there is a large girls high school, which was the palace of «Adile Sultan», sister of Sutan Abdülaziz, in the 19th century. From this point the view of the Bosphorus is magnificent.

Vaniköy takes its name from Sheik Vani, a preacher in Sultan Mehmet II's time (15th c.). Above this village, an observatory and a meteorology station are located.

Çengelköy (the Anchor Village) was named after an anchor found by Sultan Mehmet II in this area. The village square with old trees and traditional cafes looks very picturesque. The large and imposing building on the shore is the military training college (Kuleli) from the 19th century.

Beylerbeyi: (duke) Beylerbeyi Palace of the 19th century, is on the shore next to the pylons of the Bosphorus Bridge. The last sultans accomodated their guests here (see page 99).

Beylerbeyi Mosque originates from the 18th century and was built in the reign of Sultan Abdülhamit I. The pink yalı «Villa Bosphorus», which has a lovely garden, and is now visited by tourists, is located near the mosque.

By the seashore, we see the largest and most impressive yalı of all the old yalıs, the «Red Yalı» of Mustafa Emin Paşa (18th c.)

Kuzguncuk (small raven) is another pretty village with small yalıs.

Üsküdar is the old Scutari, which we already know (see p. 115). Sailing past the Maiden's Tower we return to our departure station, and our ferry ride comes to an end.

The old "yalı"s (the summer mansions of the high officials)on the Asiatic shore of the Bosphorus

Yalı of "Salih Efendi"

Yalı of "Amcazade Hüseyin Paşa"

Yalı of "Kadınefendi"

Yalı of Count "Ostrolog"

The "Red Yalı"

Yalı "Villa Bosphorus"

Üsküdar and the "Iskele Mosque"

ÜSKÜDAR F4

Üsküdar is the most interesting quarter of the city on the Asiatic shore and is located right opposite the Golden Horn. The narrow sided streets with frame-houses convey the typically oriental picture of Istanbul. Üsküdar was called Chrysopolis (the City of Gold) in ancient times. Later it was named Scutari. Using Üsküdar as a jumping-off place, Xenophon led his army of 10.000 soldiers to Europe over the Bosphorus in 400 B.C. In 324 A.D. Constantine I defeated his rival Licinius here and became the absolute monarch. In the 7th and 8th centuries Üsküdar was destroyed by the Arabs and the Persians. In 1203 commanders of the Fourth Crusade occupied the town, and finally in the middle of the 14th century Üsküdar was taken by the Turks. During the Ottoman Empire the sultans developed the town as the commercial centre, and decorated it with mosques. and caravanserais. All the roads of Asia Minor ended here, and pilgrims started their yearly journey to Mecca in Üsküdar. With the construction of the Asiatic railway (1903) Üsküdar lost its old importance. Right at the harbour we see **the fountain of Ahmet III** built in the Turkish style in 1728. Behind it there is :

the Iskele Mosque or the Mihrimah Mosque, which was commissioned by Mihrimah Sultan, daughter of Suleyman the Magnificent and wife of the Grand Vizier Rüstem Paşa in 1547, to the architect Sinan. Its dome with 16 lunettes, rests on arches which open to three semi-domes.

On the side overlooking the Bosphorus there is a lobby with domes and a columned gallery with

A fruit stand in the market of Üsküdar

two minarets. Mihrab and mimber are of fine marble, whereas the doors and preacher's stool are inlaid with mother-of-pearl and ivory.

Yeni Valide Mosque F4

is located farther south. Sultan Ahmet III built it between 1708 and 1710 in the classical style and dedicated it to his mother. Gülnuş Ümmetullah (rose-drinker). Four semi -domes placed in the corners surround the main dome that rests on eight piers. Mihrab and mimber are decorated artistically. The front courtyard which is surrounded by columns, has a beautiful ablution fountain (Şadırvan) in the centre. At the corner of the mosque is the Valide's tomb (türbe) with an open dome. The old Turks gave special importance to rain, and today it's also considered God's blessing (rahmet). Probably that's the reason why his mother wanted to have an open tomb.

Şemsi Ahmet Paşa Mosque (Kuşkonmaz Ahmet Paşa Camii) F4

is located on the shore to the right of the ferry-landing. It is considered to be one of Sinan's pretty and small building complexes and was erected in 1580. Şemsi Ahmet Pasha was the grand vizier of Süleyman the Magnificent, Selim II and Murat III. The ground plan is very simple: A dome covers the square hall. It has a front courtyard with a domed gallery. Next to the mosque is the tomb of the vizier, and a medrese (Koran school) closes the two sides of the courtyard.

The Şemsi Ahmet Paşa Mosque

The old tombs in the cemetery "Karaca Ahmet"

Cemetery of Karaca Ahmet F5

One of the largest Islamic cemeteries in the world is located above Üsküdar. Since the deceased buried here rest in the same hemisphere as the prophet, this cemetery is considered very sacred. For this reason countless generations of Moslems wanted to be buried here, and as a result of this, the cemetery has reached the edge of its boundaries. The tombstones, that are placed very closely, give information about the life of the deceased and the time they lived. Sex, age, occupation and rank of that person can be found out from the form and the size of the tombstone. The old tombstones of the men are surmounted with large stone turbans, whereas those of the women are decorated with floral designs. The tombs consist of two kinds of stones: the headstone is higher than that at the foot. The sex and rank of the deceased is shown on the higher stone. Children have small tombstones. If you see a tombstone with a turban off to the side, (I have vainly searched for one for years), it means that the person was beheaded.

In the cemetery of "Karaca Ahmet" a domed structure with six columns draws our attention, the favourite horse of Sultan Mahmut I (18th c.) was buried in it.

To the south-west of the cemetery are the large **Selim Barracks** (see map F5) which consist of a building dominated by four giant towers at the corners(19th c.). In the 16th century the barracks were a palace, which was extended in the reign of Sultan Murat IV in the 17th century. In 1887 Sultan Selim III turned the palace into the present-day barracks.

Farther south, we see the former hospital, where the English nurse Florence Nightingale attended to the wounded in the Battle of the Crimea. For a long time it was used as a high school, and it has just been turned into a School of Medicine. To the south of this building is a small bay, at the shore of which stands the imposing **train station (Haydarpaşa)** in the Asian section of Istanbul. It was built by Germans in 1903 and was reconstructed in 1917 after a fire.

Kadıköy (village of the judge) F6

is located on the southern shore of the abovementioned bay. In 685 B.C. Greeks from Megara, the so-called blind, settled here. The town was an important residence of the archbishop. In 451 AD.

View of the Bosphorus by night from Çamlıca Peak

the fourth Oecumenical Council, at which the church of Constantinople earned the same privileges as Rome, took place here. The crusaders occupied the town in 1203, and since 1350 it has been under Turkish control.

Unfortunately, there are no monuments remaining from the Byzantine period in the town.

Çamlıca (The Pine Peak)

This peak is located on the Asiatic side a few kilometres away from Üsküdar. Because of the slender TV tower, we recognize this 267m-high viewpoint easily. From here we have an impressive view of the Bosphorus, the European section, the Marmara Sea and the Princes' Islands. It's recommended that you go there on a sunny day before noon when the sun is still in the east, and its rays fall on the European section and the Bosphorus itself.

The peak is visited very often in the summer. Brides in their bridal gowns also come to this popular site to have a pleasant start in their new life. Two cafés furnished in the Turkish style of the 18th century, have been serving here since the beginning of 1980.

Maiden's Tower or Leander's Tower (Kız Kulesi) E4

The 30m-high lighthouse is located 180m off the Asiatic shore of the Bosphorus. It marks the border between the Bosphorus and the Sea of Marmara.

At around 500 B.C. a customs station was already standing here. Later the Byzantines built a small castle, from which a chain was linked to the old city and stretched to block the Bosphorus. Today's tower dates to the year 1763. The Turkish name «Kız Kulesi» is derived from an old legend: A sultan had a daughter, whose fate was foretold that she would die from the bite of a serpent. To protect her, her father kept her in this tower. She was eventually bitten by the serpent, smuggled out to the islet in a fruit basket.

The European name «Leander's Tower» originates from the myth between the Priestess of Artemis Hero and her lover Leander, who drowned there in his attempt to swim the strait to see her. Actually, he was crossing the Dardanelles between Sestos and Abydos.

The book «Of the Sea and the Love Waves» written by Franz Grillpazer refers to this legend.

"Leander's Tower" with Topkapı Palace in the background

The Princes' Island "Büyükada"

The Princes' Islands (Adalar)

These are the islands located 19-28km off Istanbul in the south-eastern part of the Marmara Sea. Ferries departing from Sirkeci reach the islands in 55-80 minutes.

This archipelago consists of four big and inhabited islands, and five smaller and uninhabited ones. The ferry stops only at the four islands. In antiquity they were called People's Islands, in Byzantine times they were named Priests' Islands because of the countless cloisters on the islands, and the ferruginous colour of the stones made the Turks describe them as Red Islands (Kızıl Adalar).Only a century ago did they become popular as a resort and as a place to bathe. Monks and fishermen used to live there.Since they are close to the city, and there is a scheduled ferry connection, the Princes' Islands are favourite resorts today. Apart from the garbage trucks, police cars and fire trucks there is no traffic on the islands, only horse carriages, which visitors welcome for excursions, are admitted for transportation.

The four residential islands are:

Kınalı (Dyed-with-Henna) 1.3 sq.km.

This island is the closest one to Istanbul. It's quite bare and has small bays. Kınalı gets its name from the reddish colour of its cliffs along the shore. Of the monasteries which once were prisons, only fragmentary walls remain.

Burgaz 1.5 sq.km.

Probably an ancient watchtower, which existed on its summit until the 19th century, accounts for this name (pyrogos=tower). The former residents were mostiy Greeks, and there are now different churches from that time. Burgaz has a beautiful pine forest and a lot of summer villas. Its highest point with 162 metres offers a wonderful view.

Heybeli (the Saddle-Bag Island) 2.3 sq.km.

It was originally named the Copper Island after the old copper mine on the island. The current

Carriages on "Büyükada"

name refers to its form. The Monastery of the Holy Trinity which now houses a theological school, was erected in 857 and is located on the northern hill. In the saddle of the two hills is the Naval Hospital, and to the left of the ferry-landing we see the building of a former Orthodox orphanage which was turned into the Turkısh Naval Academy in 1944. With its beautiful beach, hotels and restaurants,Heybeli has became a favourite holiday resort.

Büyük Ada (the Big Island) 5.4 sq.km.

It's the biggest and most important of the Princes' Islands and most tourists visit this island. A lot of beautiful villas, clubs and hotels attract many guests in summertime, when the island becomes overcrowded. Two hills dominate the island. Each one has a monastery: To the north on "Isa Tepe" the is Monastery of Christ, and to the south on "Yüce Tepe" is the old monastery of St. George, from where we enjoy an impressive view of the sea.

The five uninhabited isles are:

Sedef Ada (the Mother-of-Pearl Island)

This isle is only inhabited during summertime. There are a few pretty villas on it. Since the ferry doesn't stop here, motor boats provide transportation between Sedef Ada and Büyük Ada in summer.

Yassı Ada (the Flat Island)

Today we see the remains of the old monasteries and the ruins of the palace of the English Ambassador Sir Henry Bulwer (1857). In 1960 the overthrown minister was imprisoned in the new building we see in front of the ruins.

Sivri Ada (the Pointed Island)

In 1910 thousands of stray dogs were brought here.

Kaşık Ada (the Spoon Island)

It's located opposite the ferry-landing of "Heybeli". This island takes its descriptive name from its form.

Tavşan Ada (the Rabbit's Island)

It's located to the south and is the smallest island in the group.

GENERAL INFORMATION

❑ Foreign Exchange

Money can be exchanged at the offical currency rate at the international borders, banks, most hotels, larger restaurants and stores.
The banks are open monday to friday 9:00-12:00 and 13:30-17:00. Euro-cheques and traveller's cheques are accepted.

❑ Important adresses

Emergency: Tel. 155   First-aid doctor: Tel. 112

❑ Consulates

*Consulate General of the United States of America Meşrutiyet Cad. 104-108 Tepebaşı Tel. 251 36 02
*Consulate General of the United Kingdom Meşrutiyet Cad. 34 Tepebaşı Tel. 251 60 81
*Consulate of Switzerland
Hüsrev Gerede Cad. 75 Teşvikiye Tel. 259 1115
*Consulate of the Netherlands
İstiklal Cad. Beyoğlu 393 Tel. 251 50 30/32

❑ Hospitals (english spoken)

*The American Hospital (American Hastanesi) Nişantaşı Güzelbahçe Sokak Tel. 231 40 50
*The German Hospital (Alman Hastanesi) Sıraselviler Cad. 110 Tel. 251 71 00

❑ Pharmacies (eczane)

Most of the west European medicaments in Turkey are producting with licence. Salable products are often to get without prescription.
The pharmacies are open on weekdays between 9:00-13:00 and 14:00-19.00.

❑ Telephone

You can make phone calls to the west European countries, from all post offices and most hotels, with a special token called jeton or a phone card.
The country codes are:

U.S.A. 001
England 0044
Switzerland 0041
Netherlands 0031

❑ The voltage

It is generally 220v. In the old section of Istanbul there are a few hotels that have 110v. The power outlets are always marked with the voltage level.

❑ The drinking water

The tap water in Istanbul is chlorinated and can be safely used; but also bottled spring water (şişe suyu) and mineral water with carbondioxide (soda) are recommended.

❑ The restrooms

They are mostly identified with male and female symbols.
Ladies = kadın or bayan
Men = erkek or bay

❑ The time

Istanbul keeps the same East-European time, as as in all of Turkey. It's one hour ahead of Central European countries such as Germany, Austria, Switzerland and the Netherlands.
Turkey observes the extra hour of daylight saving between 30 March and 25 October.

❑ Holidays

Official Holidays

January 1st	New Year's Day
April 23rd	Independence and Children's Day
May 19th	Youth and Sport's Day
August 30th	Victory Day
October 29th	Republic Founddation Day

❑ Religious Holidays

Şeker Bayramı	Ramadan Holiday (lasts 3 days)
Kurban Bayramı	Sacrificial Holiday (lasts 4 days)

The dates of these holidays are 10 days earlier every year according to the Islamic calender.
n Il cambio

❑ Dining

In the world gastronomy list, the Turkish Cuisine comes third following the French Cuisine and the Chinese Cuisine.

A few tasty and interesting dishes are as follows:

Soups

Düğün Çorbası	"The Wedding Soup" with yoghurt and rice
Balık Çorbası	Fish soup
İşkembe Çorbası	Tripe soup thickened with egg

Salads

Çoban salatası	"Shepherd's Salad" with tomatoes,cucumbers, olives and onions
Cacık	Cucumber in yoghurt sauce (with garlic)

Meat dishes

Döner kebab	Mutton grilled on a vertical moving spit
Izgara köfte	Grilled meat balls
Şiş kebab	Pieces of mutton or calf on spits
Kuzu dolma	Lamb stuffed with rice and raisins
Kadın budu köfte	"Lady's Thigh", fried meat and rice balls
Biber dolması	Peppers stuffed with rice and ground beef
Domates dolması	Tomatoes stuffed with rice and ground beef
Kabak dolması	Stuffed zucchini
Karnıyarık	"Split Belly"(Eggplant stuffed with ground meat and onions)

Vegetables prepared with olive oil

Imam bayıldı	"The imam fainted from excitement" (Eggplant prepared with onions, tomatoes and olive oil)
Yaprak dolması	Grape leaves stuffed with rice
Zeytinyağlı fasulye	Green beans prepared in tomato sauce with olive oil
Zeytinyağlı enginar	Artichokes in olive oil

Fish dishes

Midye tava	Fried mussels
Midye dolma	Mussles stuffed with rice and raisins
Kılıç şiş ızgara	Grilled sword fish
Uskumru ızgara	Grilled mackerel
Palamut ızgara	Grilled tunny
Lüfer ızgara	Grilled blue fish
Kalkan tava	Fried turbot
Karides güveç	Shrimps with cheese sauce baked in clay pot

Desserts

Zerde	Rice pudding with saffron
Kadın göbeği	"Lady's Belly Button"-dessert
Vezir parmağı	"Vizier's Finger", desert baked and soaked in syrup
Baklava	Puff-pastry stuffed with walnuts and pistachios
Tel kadayıf	Threaded dough stuffed with pistachios and walnuts, soaked in syrup
Revani	A dessert soaked in syrup
Dondurma	Icecream

Museum and Bazaar Hours

The Archaeological Museum: Every day from 9.30 - 17.00 except Mondays.

Museum of the Ancient Orient: Every day from 9.00 - 17.00 except Mondays.

The Tile Museum (Çinili Köşk): Every day from 9.30 - 17.00 except Mondays.

Topkapı Palace: Every day from 9.00 - 17.00 except Tuesdays.

Haghia Sophia: Every day from 9.30 - 16.30 except Mondays.

The Underground Cistern:
Every day from 9.00-17.00.

The Chora Church: Every day from 9.30 - 16.00 except Wednesdays.

The Church of the Pammakaristos: Every day from 9.30 - 16.30 except Wednesdays.

Hahia Eirene:
Closed for the time being.

The Tomb of Eyüp Ensari:
Every day from 10.00 - 16.00 except Mondays.

Dolmabahçe Palace:
Beylerbeyi Palace:
Küçüksu Palace:
These are open every day from 9.30 - 17.00 except Mondays and Thursdays.

The Military Museum: Every day from 9.00 - 17.00 except Mondays and Tuesdays.

The Naval Museum: Every day from 9.00 - 17.00 except Mondays and Tuesdays.

The Castle of "Rumeli Hisarı" and
The Citadel of "Yedikule": are open every day from 9.30 - 16.30 except Wednesdays.

The Castle of "Anadolu Hisarı":
Every day entrance free.

The Covered Bazaar and
The Egyptian Bazaar: Every day from 9.00 - 18.30 except Sundays.

The sunset in Istanbul

Turhan Can, the author of this book, was born in Istanbul on the Bosphorus. He graduated from the German Highschool in Istanbul and studied german philology and history of art at the University of Istanbul. Since 1968 he has been working as a tour guide and is an amateur-photographer. This book "Istanbul, Gate to the Orient" is his first publication.

ISTANBUL, "Gate to the Orient"

by Turhan Can

Translated by Gaye Tınaztepe

Photos: Turhan Can
Plans and illustrations: Anita and Turhan Can
Graphic: Turhan Can
Printed by: ORIENT Matbaacılık Ltd.-(0212) 418 66 81

Montage: Dinç Montaj
Type setting: Özyalçın Dizgi
Film: Ruşen Grafik
Text editing: Anita Gilett

Sirkeci Kastel İş Merkezi B Blok Kat 5 No. 134 ISTANBUL
Tel. (0212) 268 22 47 - (0212) 511 65 35 fx.(0212) 270 37 37

www.orientpublic.net e-mail: orientpublic@tnn.net

Published by ORIENT Ltd. Co.

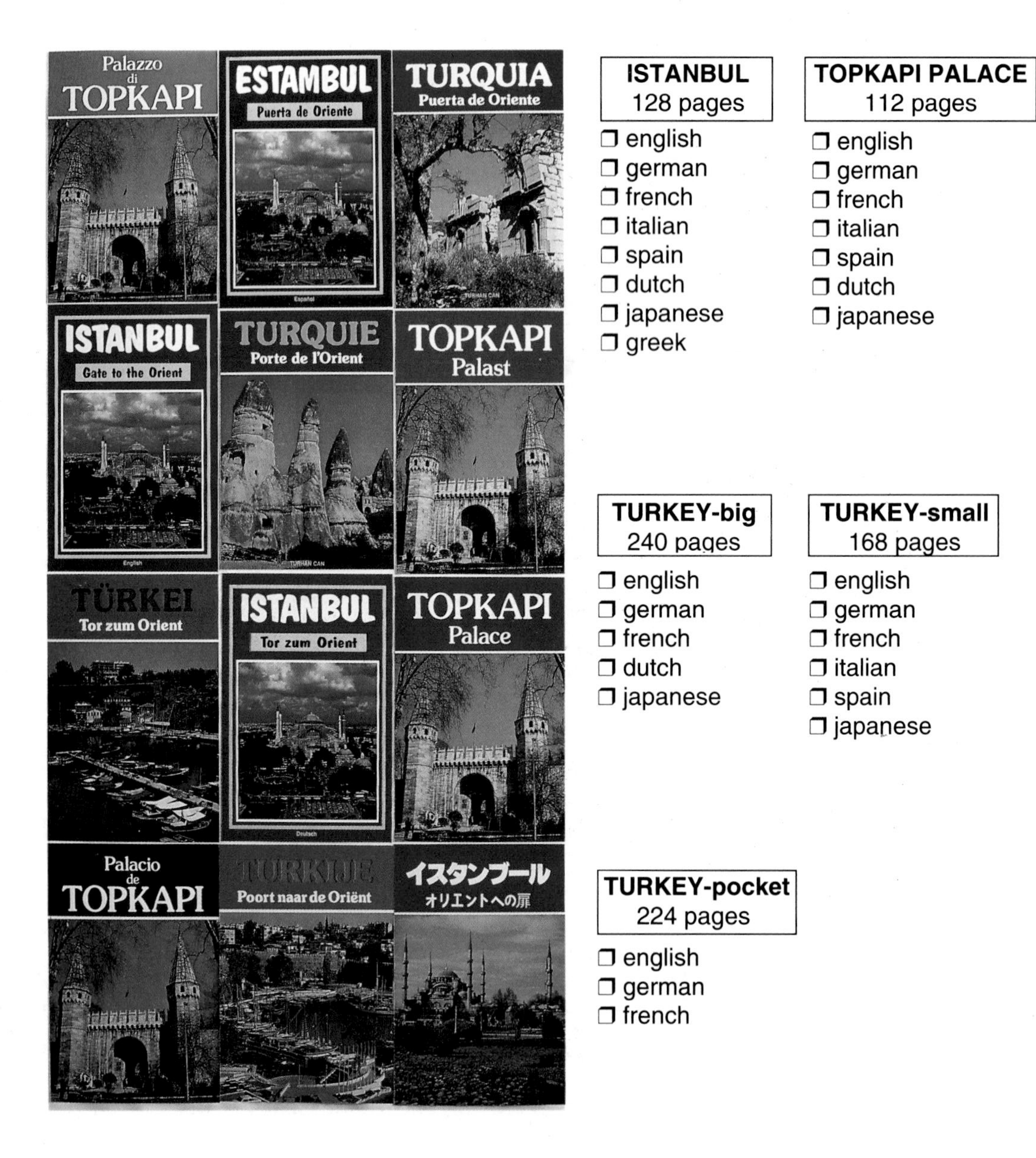

ISTANBUL
128 pages

- ❒ english
- ❒ german
- ❒ french
- ❒ italian
- ❒ spain
- ❒ dutch
- ❒ japanese
- ❒ greek

TOPKAPI PALACE
112 pages

- ❒ english
- ❒ german
- ❒ french
- ❒ italian
- ❒ spain
- ❒ dutch
- ❒ japanese

TURKEY-big
240 pages

- ❒ english
- ❒ german
- ❒ french
- ❒ dutch
- ❒ japanese

TURKEY-small
168 pages

- ❒ english
- ❒ german
- ❒ french
- ❒ italian
- ❒ spain
- ❒ japanese

TURKEY-pocket
224 pages

- ❒ english
- ❒ german
- ❒ french

TOURISTIC PUBLISHING & SERVICE LTD.
ORIENT TURİSTİK YAYINLAR VE HİZMETLER LTD. ŞTİ
Sirkeci Kastel İş Merkezi B Blok Kat 5 No.134-139 Istanbul - TURKEY
Tel. 0212-511 65 35 fax. 0212-270 37 37
www: orientpublic.com e.mail: orientpublic@turk.net